Leaving a Legacy

Turn Your Family Tree into a Family Book

By Rebecca Shamblin

 Life Remembered Press

ISBN 979-8-9893228-0-0

www.rebeccashamblin.com

First Edition

Printed in the United States of America

Cover art elements by ilonitta and Freepik

Disclaimer: This book does not replace the advice of a legal professional. Consult your lawyer before publishing images that do not belong to you.

Adobe®, *Adobe Photoshop®*, and *Adobe Photoshop Elements®* are registered trademarks of Adobe Systems Incorporated.

Charting Companion® is a trademark of Progeny Genealogy Inc.

FamilySearch® is a trademark of the Genealogical Society of Utah.

Family Book Creator® is a trademark of Stefan Harms.

Family Tree Maker® is a registered trademark of The Software MacKiev Company.

Google Maps® is a trademark of Google Corporation.

Microsoft Word® is a registered trademark of Microsoft Corporation.

PDF-XCHANGE® is a trademark of PDF-XChange Co Ltd.

Introduction

*Dedicated to the members of the
Family Book Creator User Group on Facebook*

Your support and enthusiasm have been priceless.

CONTENTS

INTRODUCTION

Creating family history books is the culmination of over twenty years of genealogical research for me. I can't tell you how satisfying it is to hold a physical book in your hands, safely guarding your hard work for generations to come. Computer hardware and software evolve, and we have all experienced the heartbreak of a corrupt file or a mysterious error holding our data hostage. Modern technology is essential for research, but good old-fashioned paper and ink is just as critical. We need that physical legacy.

However, taking years of research and trying to turn it into a cohesive narrative is no simple task. It is easy to feel over-whelmed and

Figure 1: My second family history book

put it off until next year, especially if you feel the burden of ancestral honor, and want to do "right" by your family.

But you *can* do this. I have produced multiple family history books, and I am here to hold your hand through the process.

This is your year to finally bring everything together. It won't be long before you are sitting down with your grandchildren to page through the story of your family.

SUMMARY OF THE PROCESS

In this book you will learn to:

1. Collect and organize your research using genealogy software.
2. Write illustrated biographies for each couple.
3. Produce a polished final document.
4. Get your book professionally printed.
5. Share your masterpiece.

HELPFUL TOOLS

I used the following tools in my process, but the only critical one you need is Word or an equivalent word processing software.

Illustrated examples in this book will pull primarily from these tools but should hopefully be universal in application. For example, I will explain how to insert a citation in Microsoft Word, but almost any word processing software will have this same feature, and the procedure should be similar.

I am a Windows user, so any menu screenshots will be drawn from the PC version of an application. All of the programs listed here (except for PDF X-Change) have Mac versions.

Program	Category	Usage
Family Tree Maker 2019®	Genealogy software	Database "home" where research is stored and organized
Microsoft Word® 365	Word processing software	Editing software for composition and layout of the biographical chapters and the final product
Family Book Creator® 2019	Plug-in for Family Tree Maker (FTM)	Plug-in to pull everything together and create the structure of the book, the family tree charts, the data summaries, and the indexes
Charting Companion 8®	Plug-in for FTM	Plug-in to generate a 7-generation fan chart
PDF X-Change® Editor	PDF software	Software to add background graphics to every page and export the document to PDF
Adobe® Photoshop® CC	Image editing software	Software for editing interior graphics and creating the book cover
Lulu.com	Self-Publisher	Print-on-demand service used to actually print and sell the book

Tip: If you are not familiar with the genealogical programs listed here, they both have extremely helpful user groups on Facebook: Family Tree Maker Users and Family Book Creator Users.

BARRIERS TO SUCCESS

Chances are high that this isn't the first time you have contemplated writing a family history book. Maybe this has been a secret dream for years. If so, this is a solid opportunity for you to be honest with yourself about what has prevented you from reaching that goal so far. In order for you to find success in this project, you will eventually need to:

STOP RESEARCHING

The hardest part is knowing when to stop researching and start writing. You will never feel "done" researching your family tree. One of the great joys of genealogy is the comforting feeling that there is there is always more to find. At some point, you need to draw a line in the sand and declare that the research phase is over (or at least paused).

STOP PROCRASTINATING

Your brain may protest that now is not a good time – maybe next month or next year. But you must set a deadline for yourself and stick to it, or the years will simply slip away. If you are writing for an elderly relative, it is even more important to get moving, because time is precious. There is always a reason to put this off, so be firm with yourself.

STOP OVERTHINKING

You may feel a great pressure to "do right by your ancestors" by honoring them with a great magnum opus. If you are convinced that your book has to be the pinnacle of genealogical writing, you will talk yourself out of getting started every time. It doesn't need to be perfect … it just needs to be done.

If none of this convinces you, think about the fleeting nature of digital information. The sooner you have your research in printed form, the less devastating a hard drive crash or web business failure will be (what would happen to your research if Ancestry.com went out of business tomorrow?). Software and filetypes evolve, but a printed tree will always be readable.

Write what you have for now. You can always go back and do a second edition someday, but not until your first edition is completed.

PHASE 1: PLANNING

1

Planning can seem like the greatest obstacle for some people because it involves making so many high-level decisions that feel as if they have great consequences. But planning is an essential part of the process. You cannot start work until you know what you are working on.

BOOK STRUCTURE

ANCESTOR VS. DESCENDANT

Do you want your focus to be on the past and sharing the origins of your family? Or do you want to trace the descendants of a specific family or surname and see where everyone is today? Or both?

I decided to focus on ancestors for now. That is where my real interest lies, because I enjoy solving mysteries and tracing family lines through very old documents.

Plus, ancestry does not come with complicated questions of data privacy, which arise when living people are involved. It also means that my books will not be instantly outdated as future generations are born.

I do plan to eventually get around to descendant books after I finish the ancestor ones, but I have many years before I reach that point.

PRIVACY

Privacy is always going to be a complex issue. If you are writing this book for yourself or a few siblings, it is probably not a significant risk. If you distribute it in person (e.g., at family reunions) that makes it less complicated as well, since you know the recipients.

But if you are making your book available for purchase online, I would caution against descendant books (at least ones reaching to the most recent decades). There are many reasons people choose to keep their information private, and it would be a huge task to contact each person in your book to obtain their permission.

WHO ARE YOU WRITING ABOUT?

Who is at the base of the family tree for your book, or who is at the top of it?

CHOOSING A ROOT PERSON

The natural choice for the root person in your book might be you – after all, you are the person who ties it all together. This might be the right answer for many people, but it was not right for me.

Here are some questions you might ask yourself:

- **What is the scope of work I am comfortable with?**
  - o Making one of your parents the root person instead of you will cut the workload (and page count) for this particular book in *half*. Making your grandparent the root person instead will cut that half in half again. And so on.

- **How soon do I want to be done?**
  - o Reducing the scope also brings the finish line closer. Are you someone who needs the satisfaction of completing a task fairly quickly to avoid boredom? Do you want that emotional validation in the next year or two? If so, be realistic about the time investment required to meet that goal.

- **What time period do I want to explore?**
  - o For me, I wanted to write about my first-generation ancestors, my immigrant ancestors, and those in the ancestral "home" in Europe. Mathematically, that worked out to making my great-grandparents the root people, since they were mostly second-generation Americans.

- **How large of an audience am I aiming for?**
  - o If you only want to write a book for your siblings, making your parents the root is a perfect idea. If you're hoping to catch the interest of second and third cousins, you may want to shift back a few generations. This way they can purchase only the content related to their specific family line.

Overall, the primary driver in this decision for me was project scope. Focusing on one great-grandparent at a time allowed me to work swiftly and achieve my first goal in less than 15 months. That was so satisfying and encouraging that I jumped right into my second book.

Once you have selected the starting generation, you can select the actual ancestor. I decided to start with my paternal grandmother's parents, because she is still with me, and I knew how much she would value a book like this.

You might choose one ancestor over another just because you have more content for them, or because you are taking a trip to their homeland next year, or simply because they seem the most fun to work with. It is all up to you.

WHAT IS A GENERATION?

For the purposes of my book, I decided that **a generation starts when the person leaves the family home**, usually when they get married. A non-marriage "leaving home" milestone could also be military service, solo immigration, or taking up an occupation.

So in my book, anything happening during Charles Schmidt's childhood can be found in his parents' chapter. Anything happening after his wedding is found in Charles' own chapter.

You can also use this framework for organizing files and photos by having one folder per couple, starting with their wedding.

Some exceptions to this:

1. I include a person's birth or baptism record in their own chapter because it just feels more intuitive to me.

2. If they are in the final generation of the book and I know I will not have a chance to write separately about their childhoods, I will include a little more about their family and upbringing.

CHOOSING THE NUMBER OF GENERATIONS

I did include a fourth generation in my book about my great-grandmother Olive, but I did not write full biographies for those ancestors. First, I was exhausted! By writing biographies for the first three generations, I was writing seven narrative chapters total (Olive's parents, grandparents, and great-grandparents). Had I extended back to the fourth generation, that workload would have more than doubled, leaving me with 15 biographies to write. And, as it was, my second book was over 320 pages long.

Moreover, I simply did not have enough data for those older generations to make a biography interesting. It was too long ago for photos, and foreign documents were harder for me to track down.

Sticking with three generations let me tell the story of Olive's first-generation ancestors, her immigrant ancestors, and their families back home. That was enough for my purposes. So, I included that last generation, but I stuck to the standard birth/marriage/death information that Family Book Creator generates automatically.

If I had started with my *grandmother* as my root person instead of my *great*-grandmother, I probably would have included an additional generation, because it was her *great-great*-grandparents who were the immigrants in that case. That was another reason I chose my great-grandparents as the root people for my books. This way I was telling the home country stories without needing to write 15 chapters at once.

Your choice will have to be based on your own family, the content you have access to, and the story you have in mind.

GENEALOGY SOFTWARE

As a researcher, you need a home for all your genealogical data. I highly recommend downloading software that lets you control your own tree, rather than relying on subscription services like Ancestry.com to stay in business. By making this decision at the start of your book process, you can save yourself time and energy later.

FAMILY TREE MAKER (FTM)

My favorite genealogical software by far is Family Tree Maker by The Software MacKiev Company. It is a powerful tool for research and the foundation for everything I create in my books. FTM has robust citation abilities, which support strong research practices. The way it manages media means I can attach photos and documents to multiple people and easily access whatever I need, rather than relying on an alphabetical sort of filenames in Windows Explorer.

The most powerful feature for me, however, is the built-in integration with Ancestry.com. I can easily synchronize my FTM tree with my Ancestry tree, meaning I can keep my research safe and sound on my computer, but still share it publicly. Ancestry and FamilySearch hints appear in my tree within FTM. I can find and download Ancestry records directly within FTM, which automatically creates my citations. Best of all, those images remain stored on my computer indefinitely, even if I do not continue to maintain an Ancestry subscription.

If you use other family tree software, there is always the option of exporting your tree to a GEDCOM format and importing it into FTM. You can also download your tree directly from Ancestry.com into FTM.

> Tip: You will see many references to FTM in this book, and it is required if you wish to use the Family Book Creator plug-in. However, neither are mandatory and I will make note when something in this book applies *only* to these programs.

FAMILY BOOK CREATOR (FBC)

Family Book Creator is an amazing plug-in that automatically creates books based on FTM content. A plug-in is software that you can add to existing software to extend its capabilities and features. FTM will be where your data lives, and FBC will take that data and turn it into a book for you. FTM does have a somewhat similar feature, but FBC is far more powerful and customizable.

FBC automates much of the book-making process, producing family charts, genealogical data in sentence format, citations, indexes, color-coding, photo albums, and more.

It also provides seemingly endless options for customizing the results. You can choose the level of detail as well as the individual fact types that are used. The pages below were produced by FBC in just seconds, using default settings!

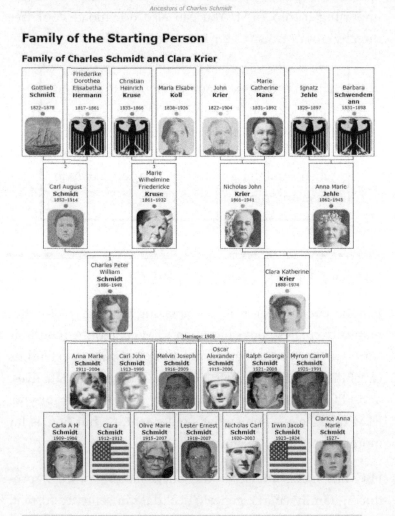

Figure 2: Sample FBC-generated page

18

PHASE 1: PLANNING

1. **Charles Peter William Schmidt** was born on Monday, September 20, 1886, in Thiensville, Ozaukee County, Wisconsin, USA.[1-4] He was the son of Carl August Schmidt (2) and Marie Wilhelmine Friedericke Kruse (3). He was also known as **Charles Schmitt**.

Charles Peter William Schmidt

His religious affiliation in Freistadt was in 1886 Lutheran.[5]

He worked as a Building tracks for the Interurban Railway in 1907.[6, 7] Charles Peter William worked as a Fireman at an electric plant in 1926.[8]

He died in Port Washington on February 24, 1949, at the age of 62.[1, 2, 4, 9] He passed away at St. Alphonsus Hospital after a short illness. Charles Peter William was buried at St. Mary's Cematary in Port Washington after February 24, 1949.[1, 2, 4]

At the age of 22, Charles Peter William married **Clara Katherine Krier** on Monday, October 19, 1908, at Witnesses were Oscar Krier and Mathilda Krier in Lake Church, Belgium, when she was 20 years old.[9-11] They had thirteen children.

Clara Katherine Krier

Clara Katherine was born in Wauwatosa, Milwaukee County, on Saturday, January 28, 1888.[9, 12, 13]

She was the daughter of Nicholas John Krier and Anna Marie Jehle. She was also known as **Clara Kneer**.[14]

Clara Katherine was baptized at Godparents were Fred Jehle and Maria Catherine Krier. The priest was Father Nicolaus in Holy Cross Church, Milwaukee, on January 29, 1888.[15] She received first communion at Same day as her confirmation in Lake Church, Belgium, Ozaukee County, on June 24, 1900.[16] Clara Katherine was confirmed at Same day as her first communion in Lake Church on June 24, 1900.[17]

Clara Katherine reached 86 years of age and died in Cecil, Shawano County, on August 01, 1974.[9, 12, 13, 18-22] She left behind 145 direct descendants. She was buried in Port Washington, Ozaukee County.[12, 13, 20, 22]

Children of Charles Peter William Schmidt and Clara Katherine Krier:

f   I. **Carla A M Schmidt** was born on August 22, 1909.[23] She was also known as **Miss Carla Schmidt**.[24, 25]

Carla

Carla A M died on June 17, 1986, at the age of 76.[26]

She was buried in Wauwatosa, Milwaukee County.[23]

Figure 3: Sample FBC-generated page

Note that there are multiple instances of awkward phrasing that require tweaking of default settings. For example, text in my Description field has been inserted before my Place field ("Clara Katherine was baptized at Godparents were Fred Jehle …"). This can be adjusted within FBC by telling it to place Description as its own sentence after Place, or fixed manually in Word after running FBC.

FBC also has the extremely useful ability to seamlessly incorporate individual Word documents and PDF files among the rest of the pages it produces. This means you can make use of its automated features and still write your own narrative biographies for each couple. FBC will then bring everything together for you. It even sequentially numbers figures and citations regardless of whether they come from FBC-generated text or from an added document.

It is entirely possible to produce a quality family history book by manually gathering information and compiling a book. I will certainly be describing that process here. However, I firmly believe the entire project will be much easier, faster, and of higher quality if you are able to use FBC.

This software is so powerful that it was the sole reason I selected FTM when choosing genealogical software. Both FTM and FBC have a one-time cost, so they will not add any monthly subscriptions to your budget. Be sure to ask your local genealogical society if they have FTM/FBC discounts.

You do not have to commit to using FBC at this point in the process, but if you think you might, you will want to use FTM during the research phase. That's why it is helpful to consider this option early on, so you don't have to convert to different software halfway through.

CHOOSING A PRINTING SOLUTION

I recommend choosing your printing company before you ever start writing. Different companies offer different options, and you would hate to spend months laying out a beautiful 8.5"x11" document only to discover your printing company only offers up to 8x10".

PRINTING AT HOME

There are certain benefits to using your own desktop printer. It is easy and familiar, so there is no intimidation factor. You can print as you go, rather than having to complete the whole book before you start printing it out. And it is very simple to add or replace a single page later on if you are using a 3-ring binder.

However, home printing can be very time-consuming – as well as ink-consuming (especially if you have images in your book). And I don't know about you, but my printer just stops functioning at the most incovenient moments.

Plus, the result does not have the same polished look that professional printing can bring, especially if you are including photos. If you intend to make additional copies of your book, doing so yourself one at a time and distributing them can be an arduous process. For these reasons, I decided to use what is called "print-on-demand."

PRINT-ON-DEMAND

In years past, the traditional model of self-publishing a book required you to order a certain number of copies, often 100-500 books, and sell them yourself. I did not want to have the hassle of collecting money from family members and shipping each book myself all over the country. And I really did not want to be stuck with a bunch of unwanted books left over at the end if I overestimated demand.

The "print-on-demand" (POD) model allows you to order one book at a time. The cost per book is higher, but it is worth it for me. Many POD companies also allow you to make the ordering website available to anyone, so you can send that link to your relatives. They can order it themselves, pay the printing company directly, and have the book shipped straight to their home without ever involving you.

In practice, I do find that some relatives reach out to have me order for them, because the technology can be a little confusing for them or they don't trust online ordering. But it is still a better strategy for me overall.

This practice also allows me to create multiple versions of the same book. I have the full-color hardcover version of my book at full price and a black & white paperback version at a lower price point.

WHAT TO LOOK FOR IN A PRINTING COMPANY

As you research printing companies, there are a few questions you should be asking:

1. What book dimensions do they offer?
2. Do you like the cover options?
3. Do they have responsive customer service?
4. What kind of turnaround time do they offer?
5. Is there a minimum number of copies to be ordered?
6. What is the price for each copy?
7. What distribution options are available?
8. What kind of commission does the printer collect when selling to others?
9. What is the quality of the printing? How thick are the pages? Does the ink "bleed" through?
10. How user-friendly is the website interface?

LULU.COM

I did quite a bit of research in 2021 and decided to use Lulu.com. I tried other printing companies as well, but I was not happy with their print quality or their customer service. I needed someone who responded to my concerns in days, not weeks.

Why did I choose Lulu? Primarily because they were taking the smallest commission for private distribution. I wanted to make my book for sale to my grandma's cousins and other descendants. Many other publishers wanted 40-60% of my total sales! I was going to have to price the books way too high for that, so I turned to Lulu, where the commission for independent distribution was only 20% of sales.

Please note that Lulu's commission rate for *global* distribution, such as through Amazon.com, is much higher and more in line with Lulu's competitors. Since I never intended to sell to a general audience, I was concerned solely with the independent rate.

Lulu also offered the standard letter-sized page (8.5" x 11") that I wanted (unlike Blurb, for example, which did not).

Finally, Lulu Direct offers the ability to sell books directly through my own website, allowing greater control over the whole process.

EBOOKS

As genealogists, we spend our time finding and preserving evidence that has outlived our ancestors. Shouldn't we hope for the same after we are long gone?

There are many reasons to focus your energies on printed books. They will never become corrupted, be lost in a computer crash or company failure, or become inaccessible in outdated software. Anyone can read them, any time, with no electricity needed.

Also ... eBooks can be surprisingly complicated to format. If you have a very basic text-heavy manuscript, converting to an eBook format is complex but achievable. Word is not capable of this function, but there are other resources for this purpose (calibre is free software that will convert a Word doc for you, as will Draft2Digital, and Amazon.com has a built-in function for this). You will still likely need to spend a good deal of time tweaking the results.

However, if your book uses any sort of visual formatting, such as tables and images, creating a "reflowable" eBook (one that can be transformed on the fly for different devices and font sizes) is a very tall order. If an eBook is your final goal, I recommend writing your book natively in an appropriate software (e.g., Vellum for Macs or Atticus for PCs) rather than trying to import a Word file at the end of your process.

On the whole, sticking with the printed word is usually the simpler, more straight-forward path.

WORD PROCESSOR SETTINGS

An important part of your plan will be the layout and style of your book. You don't want to get to the end of the writing process only to realize you wish you had wider margins. Play with word processor options and figure out what looks "right" to you. If using POD, consult the printing company's guide to comply with their layout requirements.

Many of these settings should be very similar across word processor programs, but my examples will be pulled from Microsoft Word. In Word, you will mostly find these settings in the **Layout Ribbon**.

ORIENTATION

I wrote my entire first book in portrait orientation (vertically oriented, i.e. taller than it is wide). This is a common choice for family history books. At the very end, I realized that landscape was the better solution for me. I had a lot of images that were very wide (especially census scans), and I just couldn't display them large enough to read in portrait.

More importantly for me, I didn't like the visual feel of portrait orientation. I wanted my images and documents to flow organically in the text – specifically, I wanted text *next* to my images, not just above and below them. I felt the portrait layout was too blocky or resulted in the text adjacent to some of the images being too narrow for comfort.

PHASE 1: PLANNING

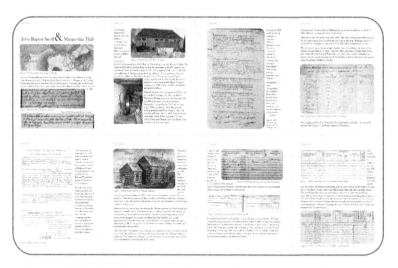

Figure 5: High-level view of example chapter in portrait orientation

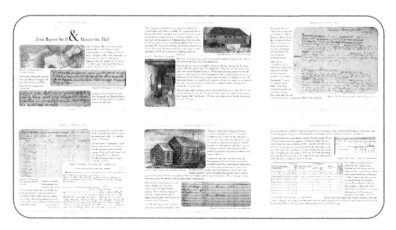

Figure 4: Final version of same chapter in landscape orientation

So, despite the tedium, I re-did every page in the narrative biographies to be landscape and changed my FBC settings (in the **Preferences** workspace, under the *Text & Page Layout* tab) and it was worth it. I could display my images as wide as I wanted, and it just felt more like a storybook to me. You, however, can make this decision from the start and save yourself some heartache. There is no right answer – it is simply a matter of your aesthetic preference.

Another appealing aspect of landscape orientation for me is that it helps the entire volume feel more like a "coffee table book," making it something special that stands out from "regular" books.

If your book is primarily text-based with few images, portrait orientation might be the best solution for you, as reading long lines of text across a horizontal page can be challenging and possibly overwhelming. If you do choose landscape in that case, consider using two columns per page (see Layout Tips on page 195).

PAGE DIMENSIONS

Because maximizing page width was important to me, I chose U.S. letter size in landscape for my dimensions (11" x 8.5"). This setting is under *Size* in the **Layout Ribbon.**

Again, there is no right answer here, but make sure to check with whatever printing company you plan to use. Lulu, my chosen printer, does offer this dimension.

BLEED

"Bleed" refers to having an extra 1/8" on every side of your page, with the intent of that area being trimmed away by the printer. If you have the default white background on each page, then you can usually ignore this step.

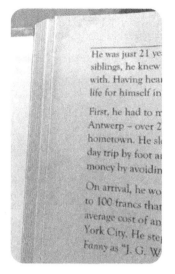

However, if you have a colored background or full-spread image that "bleeds" all the way to the edge of the page, like I did, you will need this. Without bleed, you can end up with inconsistent

Figure 6: Forgetting to include bleed

tiny slivers of white along the edges of your pages. You can see the results of this mistake here, in the thin white lines on the left edge of the pages where nothing printed.

To account for this, my Word document dimensions for the narratives and for the final manuscript were actually 11.25" x 8.75", even though the final book was 11" x 8.5".

Tip: If you use a colored or full-spread background, you will need to take special steps later to convert to a PDF. See this book's section on PDF X-Change on page 210.

MARGINS

I have experimented extensively with margins, which are largely a personal preference. I like a 1" margin on the top, 0.75" on the bottom, then 0.88" on the left and right.

You might be tempted to squeeze as much as possible onto each page, with very narrow margins, but I urge you not to do this. White space is critical to having a pleasant reading experience. Narrow margins feel crowded and claustrophobic to a reader.

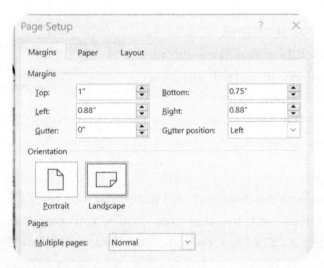

Figure 7: My margins for biographies

If you are writing your book entirely in Word, without FBC, you should turn on Mirror Margins now. Mirror margins leave more space on the side of the page that is stuck in the gutter and less space on the outer edge. If you are using most book binding methods (anything but a layflat photobook), you should use this setting.

> Tip: If you plan to use FBC, it is important *not* to turn on Mirror Margins in your individual Word biographies; instead, wait until the final edits of your fully compiled book.

After I run FBC and I'm doing final edits in my complete book document, then I turn on Mirror Margins. I take 0.25" from the outside and give it to the inside. That leaves me with 1.13" inside, and 0.63" outside margins. Make sure the sum total of your left and right margins from *before* is equal to the total of your inside and outside margins *now*. For example, in both of these figures, the total of the left/right and inside/outside margins is 1.76".

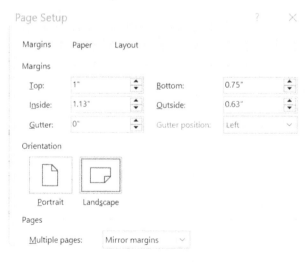

Figure 8: My margins for the final book

FONT

Font choice is very important visually. Keep your audience in mind as you choose your font style and point (size). Don't go too small, especially if your intended recipient's eyesight is not what it used to be. For main text, I like 12-14 point, and I recommend that you never go below 11 point font. These settings are under the **Home Ribbon** in Word.

Serif font styles, such as the one in this book, have decorative flourishes at the end of each letter that make the text generally easier to read. A sans-serif font is often used for headings, but I used a serif font for both the headings and text in my family book because it felt more old-fashioned.

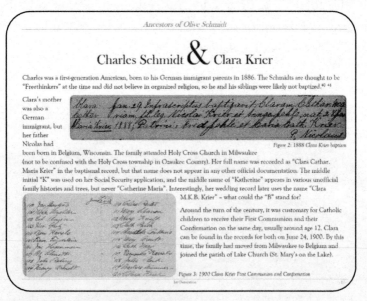

Figure 9: Font style and point in Word

I decided on Baskerville Old Face (28 point) for headings and Goudy Old Style (14 point) for my main text (I added italics for my image captions). The "&" symbol in the chapter headings is 72 point, for purely stylistic reasons.

I made my endnotes smaller (Goudy Old Style in 8 point) to take up less room, since I have so many. If you plan to use FBC, make sure that whatever endnote font you use in your Word narrative biographies matches the endnote settings you choose in FBC.

CAPITALIZATION

There is a grand tradition of capitalizing surnames in genealogy (e.g., "John SMITH and Jane DOE"). It makes content much easier to skim for researchers who are only interested in certain family lines. If your primary audience is other genealogists, I recommend you comply with this practice in your book.

However, if your primary audience is composed of family members and other non-genealogists, I would urge you to think twice. In today's society, we are accustomed to seeing text in all caps as an indicator of shouting. I worried my grandmother would envision me shouting every surname in my book, so I chose to stick with title capitalization.

There is no right or wrong answer. Just be sure you are making the decision thoughtfully and be consistent throughout your text.

ALIGNMENT

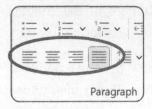

Figure 10: Alignment settings in Word

In Word, alignment settings can be found in the *Paragraph* section of the **Home Ribbon**.

Most word processors default to left-aligned text, meaning that text is lined up evenly along the left margin of the page, but there is a "ragged" edge on the right because the words on each line need different amounts of horizontal space.

> Lorem ipsum dolor sit amet, consectetur adipiscing elit. Nulla ornare viverra ligula. Sed urna dui, luctus a eros sed, iaculis porttitor erat. Sed varius, lacus sed mattis condimentum, tortor massa ultricies est, nec cursus tortor mi quis nisi. Suspendisse vitae rhoncus sem. Morbi varius sodales nisi, sed aliquet diam.

Figure 11: Left-aligned text

You can keep this alignment if you choose, but you also might consider using justified text, the way many professional books do. The word processor will automatically spread out the words on each line so that the text lines up evenly on both the left and right sides of the page.

Occasionally, using justified alignment can produce lines of text that are too widely spaced, especially when using narrow columns.

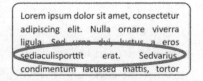

Figure 12: Oddly justified text

I prefer to handle this by either rewording, or by adding an optional hyphen at an appropriate breaking point in the first word of the following line.

Place the cursor where you want a hyphen and hit Ctrl+- (hyphen). Word will add a temporary hyphen, which will hopefully allow the first half of the word to join the line above and solve the spacing problem.

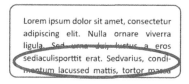

Figure 13: Adjusted justified text

Why not a regular hyphen? Because if you ever go back and edit the text such that the hyphen is not needed (because that word is now entirely on a single line), the hyphen will look very strange, and you may not notice in time to delete it.

Word does have an automatic hyphenation option, found in the *Page Setup* section of the **Layout Ribbon**. I personally find it to be very sensitive, and feel it adds more hyphens than I am comfortable with. There is also a manual hyphenation option that allows you to make a decision about each suggested hyphenation, one at a time.

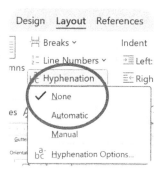

Figure 14: Automatic hyphenation in Word

If, like me, you have "control issues" but are also too impatient to evaluate every hyphen suggestion that Word offers, you might prefer my ad-hoc method, in which I only intervene when the word spacing seems egregious.

PHASE 2:
RESEARCH

2

RESEARCH TIPS

Being organized from the start can save you heartache down the road. Have a plan in place for storing and organizing the content you collect for your book.

CREATING A RESEARCH PLAN

To avoid the pitfalls of "research as procrastination," make a research plan for yourself. Decide what kind of content you are going to collect and how much of it, as well as how long this phase will last.

You don't necessarily need to finish researching the entire book before you start writing. Some people choose to research one couple (one chapter) at a time. This can help provide more variety of experience for your brain if you tend to get bored when working on the same task for too long.

It also allows you time and experience to learn the "tricks of the trade," showing you what additional research you might want in the future. For example, you might not realize until you start writing that you wish you had collected death certificates for each person. Writing one chapter at a time allows you to discover this early on.

I personally complete basic research for everyone at the start, then dig more deeply as I write each couple's chapter.

FILENAMES

When saving files during the research phase, choose a naming format and stick to it. Many people use surnames as the first element in a filename, with a goal of grouping families together when sorting alphabetically. For example, "WATRY, John family photo – 1895" and "WATRY, John US Census – 1900".

However, this model somewhat fails when working with photos of people from multiple families, as the file will only be sorted with the first surname. A file named "WATRY, John and STREFF, Robert in the cornfield – 1910" will be easily found among other Watry photos, but must be manually searched for when seeking photos of Robert Streff.

This model also doesn't allow for chronological sorting. All of the family's census records would be grouped together, for example, rather than each one being grouped with photos from a similar time period. I prefer to write chronologically, so this naming rubric would require me to jump back and forth in a very inconvenient way.

A better method for grouping family photos is to attach them to the corresponding people in genealogy software. This way, a single photo can be quickly located for any of its subjects using filters.

Since I use that method, I prefer to primarily sort my photos by date, by making the year the first element in my filenames. This way, a person's media always appears chronologically within my genealogy software. In the combined media folder of my software, records like census data from the same year (for multiple families) are also automatically grouped.

I have created the following naming convention:

Year SURNAME, FirstNames – Source YearOfCollection

Year – This is the year the original document or photo was created. If I don't know the exact year, I will add a "c" for "circa" (e.g., "1892c"). The "c" is added after the year instead of before it, so that the photo will still be sorted with other 1892 images. If I don't even have a good guess on the year, I will make my best guess as to the decade and add an "s." For example, "1890s." This format ensures that the files remain chronologically sorted. For photos after 1900, I add the full date (when known) as YYYY-MM-DD ("1975-05-24").

SURNAME, FirstNames – This is either the patriarch for family photos or the person on the far left of the photo. I will then add additional people from left to right, continuing to capitalize surnames. I start with the front row ("FR") and then identify the back row ("BR") (e.g., "1937 KRIER, Nic and Anna JEHLE fam - FR Clara, Nic, Anna, Alex BR Carl, Ernie, Bertha, Edwin, John, Otto"). When there are multiple rows, I will sometimes use "1R," "2R," etc.

Source – Where I found the content. That may be the name of whomever who sent me the file, or a website, or both (e.g., "Ancestry JohnDoeUser"). Remember not to include periods in the filename if your source was a website.

YearOfCollection – The year I found or received the content.

Whatever naming convention feels right to you, make sure to stick with it. Include as much source information as you can as a favor to your future self. It may not seem likely right now, but you are bound to forget where you found that amazing new photo.

> Tip: Having your own naming convention can be handy in quickly evaluating whether Ancestry.com is presenting you with a "new" photo hint that is actually one of your own files, re-uploaded by someone else. Unless of course you write a book sharing your convention with the world.

FILENAME LENGTH

Be aware that some genealogical software (including FTM) can become unstable if very long filenames are used. For this reason, I try to keep filenames as short as possible. I frequently abbreviate surnames when they are repeated within the filename (e.g., "1930s FEYEREISEN, John with Lena BIRENBAUM, Lawrence FEY, and Peter BIR").

I also use nicknames for first names. When pressed, I will delete spaces between names and rely only on commas (e.g., "1917c WATRY BR Kate,Marie,Barb,Jac,John,Liz,Pete FR Lar,Clara,Mary WEILAND,Fran,Mike,Dom,Frank").

FILE PROPERTIES (WINDOWS)

A more detailed way to record source information for an image would be to use File Properties. This method gets around the problem of long file names.

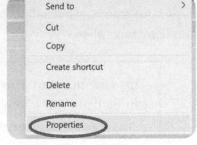

From Windows Explorer, right-click on the file and then click on *Properties* at the bottom of the menu options.

Figure 15: File Properties in Windows Explorer

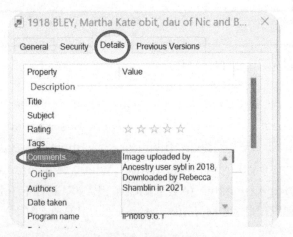

Figure 16: Comments in File Properties

When the Properties window opens, it will show the *General* tab. Look to the right and click on the *Details* tab. From there, find the *Comments* field and double-click the blank area to its right, under *Value*. This will open a text field so you can type in details about where and when you found the image and any copyright or attribution information.

You can include source information in both ways by including key details in the filenames and then fleshing them out with more detail in the Properties.

Again, the more you record, the better off you will be in the future. I only wish I had followed these conventions when beginning my research. There have been many occasions in which I wished to investigate a document further, only to realize that I no longer knew where I had found it.

COMMENTS IN THE DESCRIPTION FIELD (FTM)

The Comments field is also helpfully displayed in Family Tree Maker. If you follow the process above for recording

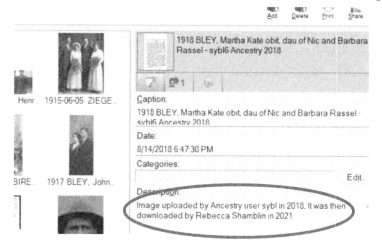

Figure 17: Viewing comments in FTM

43

source information in File Properties, FTM will display that information in the Description field when viewing the image in the **Media** workspace.

> Tip: This is a one-way process. FTM *reads* data from the file, but it does not *write* data. If you add or edit text in the Description field in FTM, it will not appear in the Comments field of File Properties.

USING GENEALOGY SOFTWARE

Whether you use Family Tree Maker or some other software, there are practices you can adopt to ensure consistency and quality results in the end. Setting good habits from the start builds a strong foundation for your final project.

CLEAN YOUR EXISTING DATA

You can only create a strong book with strong data, so take some time to clean up all the names, dates, places, and descriptions in your tree before you start.

Things to check:

1. Do you have sources listed for every fact?
2. Does every person have a profile picture specified and cropped, if available?

3. Have you capitalized all surnames consistently?
4. Have you been consistent in saying "about" or "around" for estimated dates?
5. Have you been consistent in the information included in description fields, such as witnesses to marriages, or age at time of death?

Does it need to be perfect? Certainly not. And don't let this step be a complete roadblock in starting your book. If it feels overwhelming, do a cursory skim and move on. **Any book is better than no book.** If the thought of checking all your data stops you from doing anything, it is not worth it.

OR START OVER

When I embarked on my first project, it coincided with the decision to start my family tree over from scratch. For 19 years, I had been randomly adding "facts" from all over the Web, without bothering to record sources or verify anything. I blindly accepted every "hint" I received, and merged GEDCOM files from strangers without question.

As a result, my tree had bizarre features like children born before their mothers and people getting married at age five. In short, my tree was a mess. I tried

Figure 18: My adorable first family tree website, with 4,672 people and a grand total of 5 sources

to fix it, but ultimately decided that starting fresh would actually be less work.

I installed FTM and started a new tree, only entering in data that had solid sources (beginning with the ancestors in my first book). I have been carefully building that tree ever since. I feel confident about every piece of information in there, which is a great feeling. That clean data helped create a solid book from the start.

> Tip: Remember that if you do decide to start a new tree, you are not really starting from scratch. You have all the assumed facts from your previous tree, which is a basis for tracking down evidence to support them. It is far easier to prove an alleged birth date than it is to dig up a birth date in the first place.

ENTER NEW DATA

As you collect each piece of evidence, carefully enter it into your genealogy database and make sure to create a citation so that you know where the data came from. This will help your future self if you ever need to go back and verify or expand the information, as well as help fellow researchers who want to follow in your footsteps.

ADDING MEDIA (FTM)

When adding documents such as baptism certificates, I attach my document scans to citations, using the *Media* tab in the FTM *Source Citation* window, rather than attaching them directly to people. This helps ensure that I know where each document came from.

Because of this, direct attachments to people in my tree are usually portraits and/or photos (and not documents).

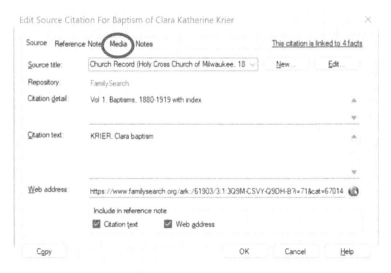

Figure 19: Source citations in FTM

When you do attach a photo with multiple subjects, make sure to attach it to every relevant person in the photo. Sometimes I attach a photo of a set of siblings to their parents in FTM, even if the parents are not depicted in the image.

USE RECOGNIZED PLACE NAMES

Place names in most genealogy programs are simply text fields, and you can enter whatever you would like. But if you want software like FTM and FBC to recognize and organize those places in an index (for example, grouping cities in the same state), you need to make sure you have "resolved" the place names. This means clarifying things like whether you meant the *town* of Milwaukee or just the *county*, or that "Belg, Oz. Cty, Wi, United States" really means "Belgium, Ozaukee, Wisconsin, USA."

RESOLVE A PLACE NAME (FTM)

How do you know if a place name is unresolved in FTM? If you view it in the **Places** workspace, it will have a little "?" next to it instead of a checkmark, and it will not be sorted in

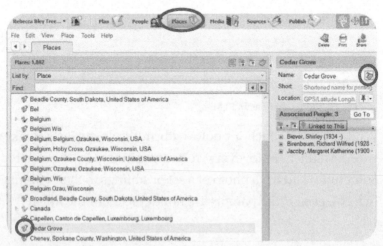

Figure 20: Places workspace

48

the proper country folder. FTM automatically collapses places by country, as you can see for the countries of Belgium and Canada here. If you don't see a hierarchy, make sure you have not toggled on "Show place names as a flat list", circled here.

Figure 21: "Place names as a flat list"

You can do this one at a time by clicking on the *?* to the right of the place name in the far-right tab. That will bring up the *Resolve Place Name* pop-up. You can search for the proper city

Figure 22: FTM Resolve Place Name window

(if you can't find your city in the official database, find the county and then type the city name in "Place detail"). Click *Replace*. After that, FTM will sort the city properly within its country, state, county, etc.

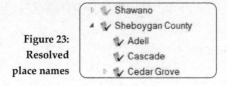

Figure 23:
Resolved
place names

RESOLVE ALL PLACE NAMES (FTM)

A faster way to do this *en masse* is select "Resolve All Place Names" from the **Tools** menu.

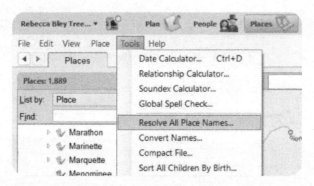

Figure 24: Resolve All Place Names in the Tools menu

FTM will offer its best guesses for each place name and you can quickly check off the correct ones. If FTM's guess is not correct, you can simply leave the default checkmark on the left and nothing will be changed.

It can be tedious to resolve your place names in FTM, but it is worth it. The Index of Places that FBC automatically creates only works if you give it good data. Having resolved places also makes it much simpler to use the **Places** features within FTM itself.

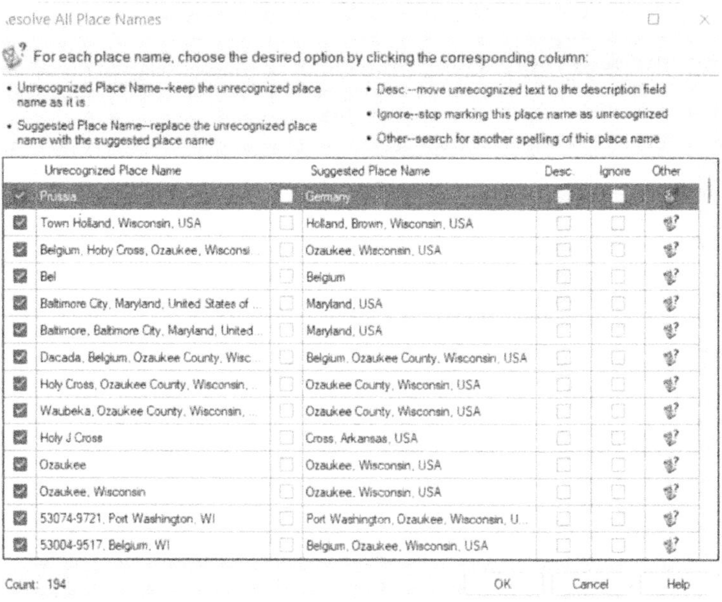
Resolve All Place Names
For each place name, choose the desired option by clicking the corresponding column:
• Unrecognized Place Name--keep the unrecognized place name as it is
• Suggested Place Name--replace the unrecognized place name with the suggested place name
• Desc.--move unrecognized text to the description field
• Ignore--stop marking this place name as unrecognized
• Other--search for another spelling of this place name
Unrecognized Place Name
Suggested Place Name
Desc.
Ignore
Other
Prussia
Germany
Town Holland, Wisconsin, USA
Holland, Brown, Wisconsin, USA
Belgium, Hoby Cross, Ozaukee, Wisconsi...
Ozaukee, Wisconsin, USA
Bel
Belgium
Baltimore City, Maryland, United States of ...
Maryland, USA
Baltimore, Baltimore City, Maryland, United ...
Maryland, USA
Dacada, Belgium, Ozaukee County, Wisc...
Belgium, Ozaukee County, Wisconsin, USA
Holy Cross, Ozaukee County, Wisconsin, ...
Ozaukee County, Wisconsin, USA
Waubeka, Ozaukee County, Wisconsin, ...
Ozaukee County, Wisconsin, USA
Holy J Cross
Cross, Arkansas, USA
Ozaukee
Ozaukee, Wisconsin, USA
Ozaukee, Wisconsin
Ozaukee, Wisconsin, USA
53074-9721, Port Washington, WI
Port Washington, Ozaukee, Wisconsin, U...
53004-9517, Belgium, WI
Belgium, Ozaukee, Wisconsin, USA
Count: 194
OK
Cancel
Help

Figure 25: Resolve All Place Names pop-up

> Tip: Resolving place names can involve a lot of data changes, so remember to compact your file frequently to avoid file corruption. If you use FTM to synchronize with a tree on Ancestry.com, update only a few places at a time and sync often to avoid failures. Always back up your FTM file before synchronizing.

CONSIDER "SHORTENED" PLACE NAMES (FTM)

FTM is rather finicky about helper geographical words in non-English languages. For example, I was writing this book for my American family, most of whom were unfamiliar with the geography of Luxembourg. I worried that using the official name of a Place in FTM (e.g., "Bertrange, Luxembourg, Luxembourg, Luxembourg") would be confusing when a canton, a district, and a country shared the same name.

However, FTM offers the "Short" field where you can type whatever descriptive name you want (even if it is longer, not shorter). I use this to spell out place names more specifically in certain cases. (e.g., "Bertrange, Canton de Luxembourg, District de Luxembourg, Luxembourg"). This feature can also help in cases where a placename has changed over time, and you wish to use the original name.

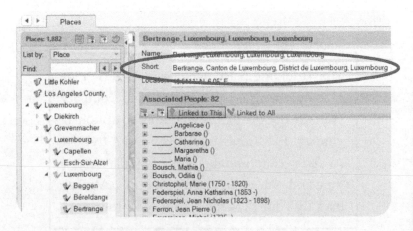

Figure 26: "Shortened Place Names" in FTM

The only exception to this rule that I have found is that FTM will allow the word "County" in the official place name, but it classifies it as a different place, so you must be consistent or you will end up with "Ozaukee County" and "Ozaukee" being two different places in FTM.

ADD COLOR CODING (FTM)

You can make use of the automatic color-coding feature in FTM to graphically illustrate each family line in your book. That way, if someone is only related to one of your family lines, they can see immediately if a section is relevant.

These colors automatically propagate to both the FBC and Charting Companion plug-ins in a very convenient way. They appear in family charts generated by FBC as well as in the indexes of the book. FBC even automatically creates a legend for them in your book introduction.

Color coding may not seem necessary when looking at an entire tree, but after reading four or five chapters of your book, a reader might be grateful to have some breadcrumbs to help remember where this couple lies in the greater tree.

To use this feature, click *Color Coding* in the upper right corner of the Tree view. You can set a specific person to a color or set all of that person's ancestors to a color (with an option to include ancestors' descendants, which I do not).

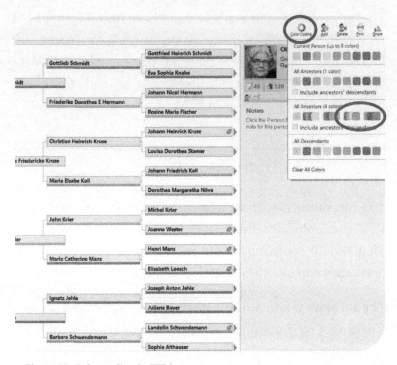

Figure 27: Color coding in FTM

You can only set four colors at a time, so you will need to do the root person's father, and then their mother separately.

> Tip: I like to use rainbow order: red/orange/
> yellow/green for father, and blue/indigo/
> purple/pink for mother. These options are
> circled in the screenshot.

WHAT TO INCLUDE IN YOUR BOOK

Most family history books provide biographical data, like birthplaces and marriage dates. But you are probably reading this right now because you want more for your book. That "more" will come in the form of context and imagery – these are the components that can turn a dry recitation of facts into a story.

BASIC DATA – BIRTH/MARRIAGE/DEATH

Basic as it is, you will still need this classic birth/marriage/death information. It is very useful to researchers and provides the overarching structure of the book itself. We build our stories around these facts.

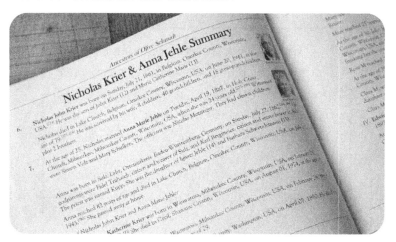

Figure 28: Basic Data in my family history book

If you find this data in someone else's tree, make sure to confirm its accuracy via primary sources, like certificates or vital records, rather than just relying on the hearsay of strangers on the internet, like my younger self did.

Although this section may not seem as exciting as other parts of your book project, it is vital. You must be confident in your foundational research, or else everything that you build upon it falls apart.

PHOTOGRAPHS

All kinds of content make a family history book useful and interesting, but *images* can make the difference between good and great. They are absolutely the eye-catching content that your readers will immediately flip through pages to see.

> Tip: Try to have at least one photograph, document, or illustration in every two-page spread, to break up huge blocks of text and provide a rest for the eyes. An unbroken "wall of text" can feel very intimidating to readers.
>
> If you don't have many images available, using pull quotes can also work to provide visual variety.

FAMILY PHOTOS

Family photos can be some of the most exciting elements in your book. Here are some of the ways you can collect photos:

- **Genealogy Websites**: Family trees on sites like Ancestry.com, MyHeritage.com, and FamilySearch.org can be a goldmine for family photos.

  o Don't just search for your own ancestor. Look up their siblings to see if other researchers have uploaded family photos but not tagged your ancestor in them.

- **Facebook**: Join groups devoted to your ancestral hometowns. Share a family portrait and some historical details, then reply to anyone who comments, asking if they have any further photos. This way you are offering something of value before asking for anything.

- Search through **closets** in the houses of your oldest relatives – or your own.

- Reach out to distant **cousins.** In large families, many family photos end up in the hands of the last child who lived at home with the parents (usually the youngest) or the one who inherited the family home.

  o Don't just ask for photos – ask if they have any ideas about who else you could ask. For example, "Hi Jane – I'm looking for old family photos. Sarah said I should ask John, and he thought that your mother might have some pictures of the reunions. If not, do you know who might have any?"

   o   Assure your family members that they can keep the photos themselves, and that you are just looking for copies or preferably scans.

- Message **DNA** matches. First, offer to share what you have. *Then* make a request from them. Expect very few people to actually reply. Do this very early in your research because sometimes it takes months if not years for people to check their messages. This is a long shot.

- Visit local **historical societies**. This is a slow, manual process with rare but thrilling rewards.

Figure 29: These five family photos all came from different sources.

Search for societies for the hometown and neighboring towns of your ancestors, for their county, for their state, or for your cultural heritage. Ask about:

   o   Donated scrapbooks or family history books
   o   Boxes of unlabeled/unindexed photos
   o   Family-name folders
   o   Newspaper archives
   o   Local real estate records

SCANS VS. PHOTOGRAPHS

Whenever needed, offer to scan photos yourself or to pay for a scanning service. Try to make it as easy as possible for people to help you.

Consider purchasing a portable scanner. I use the Canon CanoScan Lide 300. It is affordable, extremely lightweight, and easy to travel with, but it does struggle with photos larger than the surface of the scanner bed, because you cannot remove the outside frame. This means that the photograph cannot be placed directly onto the glass (it remains a few millimeters above), so the quality is reduced. Still, it is handy for items smaller than 8.5"x12".

Smartphones have also come a long way in the last several years, and I increasingly find myself relying on my phone camera rather than my scanner. It is much faster and easier to use. Lighting is the most difficult aspect of using a camera instead of a scanner. Avoid overhead lighting that creates harsh shadows and try to find a window with indirect sunlight instead.

Tip: If you are at a research center, make sure to ask permission before scanning or photo-graphing anything. Sometimes their funding comes from selling copies or scans of their content, and they may ask you to pay.

PHOTOGRAPHING PHOTOS

When trying to take a photo of a photo, keep the following guidelines in mind:

1. Turn off your flash and avoid glaring lights.

   - If you absolutely cannot avoid glare, try taking multiple shots at slightly different angles to make sure you have full coverage of the item.

2. Hold the camera directly above the photograph. This means that the edges of the photo should be parallel to the edges of the screen, not angled.

3. Choose a plain background, like an empty table.

4. If the photo is curling up, try placing a heavy ruler or book along the edges to keep it flat.

5. Hold the camera very still to avoid blur.

6. Make sure to back up your images in the cloud or on another device, in case of accident or loss.

7. If you are photographing several items in a row, check each image before moving on to the next one, to make sure everything is clearly visible.

Figure 30: Bad photo of a photo – poor lighting leading to inaccurate colors, camera is angled instead of directly above the photo, photo edges are curling up, distracting background, and camera was shaking, causing blur

Figure 31: Better photo of a photo – even lighting with true-to-print colors, camera is directly above, photo is relatively flattened, background is white, and camera was held still

MYSTERY PHOTOS

Ideally, the family photos you find will be helpfully labelled, but this is often not the case. When you don't know who is in a photo, you can try:

- Bringing the photos to the eldest relative in your family and asking for guidance. Sometimes they can't identify the person, but they can recognize signature facial features or body types within the family groups ("Oh, that must be one of Tommy's boys – look at the ears.").

- Bringing the photos to a family reunion, in an album with space to write next to each photo. Tie a pen to the album and pass it around, with a note asking for people's best guesses.

Figure 32: A photo album that I took to a reunion, with guesses and corrections added by guests

- o Or posting the photos to a family email list or social media group. Emphasize that people don't need to be certain, and that guesses are welcome.

- Bringing together all the identified photos you have, and carefully comparing faces one by one. Or enter photos into facial-recognition software and hope the technology will find similarities in the faces, which may provide clues.

- Analyzing the clothing, hairstyles, and setting to try to identify the decade in the photo, then using that information to narrow down who in the family it could be. This works best for marriage and baby photos ("Only two granddaughters were born in 1940s and only one family had an older boy, so this little baby is probably Susie Smith").

  - o The younger a person is, the easier it is to visually guess their age. When trying to visually date family portraits, start with the youngest children.

- Posting photos to relevant regional groups on Facebook and asking for help.

Include mystery photos in your book with your best guesses and caveats ("This photo likely comes from the Schmidt family and may be one of William and Selma's children, possibly on the Schmidt family farm.").

NON-FAMILY PHOTOS AND ILLUSTRATIONS

Sometimes, no matter what you do, the photos just aren't there. Maybe your family didn't have access to a camera, or maybe this time period was before photography was in general use. In that case, you still want to have some illustrations in your book. Here are some non-family images you may be able to use:

1. Old paintings and postcards of your ancestors' town
2. Photos of their church
3. Photos of old-fashioned items they might have used in their kitchen or farm
4. Photos of other houses in their town that resemble what their home may have looked like
5. Photos of what their house looks like now if you know the address
6. Photos of people wearing the traditional ethnic clothing your ancestors would have worn
7. Photos of town landmarks from a historical society
8. Paintings of military uniforms they would have worn
9. The Coat of Arms for their town or state
10. Gravestone photos
11. Contemporary maps of their country
12. Paintings of the ship they immigrated on

Figure 33: Example immigrant ship engraving

COPYRIGHT & THE CREATIVE COMMONS LICENSE

When using images, always make sure that you have permission from the copyright holder. This book does not provide legal advice. If you are uncertain about copyright permissions, please seek legal expertise. In the meantime, here are some general guidelines.

When searching the Internet for non-family photos to use, seek images that are either in the public domain or under a Creative Commons License. This means that their copyright holder will allow you to use the image, as long as you follow their rules for crediting them.

1. Go to Google Images and type in a search term.

2. Click *Tools*, then under *Usage Rights*, select *Creative Commons licenses.*

Figure 34: Usage Rights on Google Image Search

3. Click on a photo you like and look for a *License details* link. That will tell you whether and how you are allowed to use the image.

4. Make sure to take note of the Attribution section so you know how to credit the artist.

Figure 35: Google Image search result with license details

File:Ellis Island 2022 (1).JPG - Wikimedia Commons

Get this image on: **Wikimedia Commons** License details
Want to know where this information comes from? Learn more

Figure 36: Example Creative Commons license

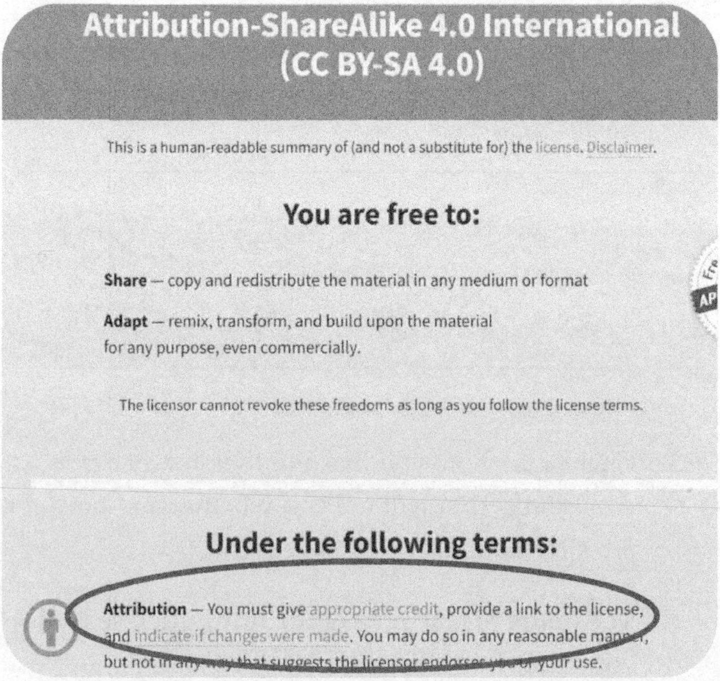

Attribution-ShareAlike 4.0 International (CC BY-SA 4.0)

This is a human-readable summary of (and not a substitute for) the license. Disclaimer.

You are free to:

Share — copy and redistribute the material in any medium or format

Adapt — remix, transform, and build upon the material
for any purpose, even commercially.

The licensor cannot revoke these freedoms as long as you follow the license terms.

Under the following terms:

Attribution — You must give appropriate credit, provide a link to the license, and indicate if changes were made. You may do so in any reasonable manner, but not in any way that suggests the licensor endorses you or your use.

DOCUMENTS

Here are some documents you might use in your books:

1. Birth/baptism records
2. Death/funeral records
3. Marriage records
4. Census records
5. Newspaper mentions
6. Naturalization records
7. Passenger manifests
8. Military draft cards
9. Real estate records
10. Wills/probate records
11. Agricultural schedules
12. School programs and report cards
13. Funeral cards

Remember to look for witnesses to civil and religious records. They were usually family members and friends and provide additional color to the facts.

> Tip: As with photographs, make sure you have the copyright holder's permission to add document scans to your book. Some archives have rules about where and how you can use the images they provide. If you cannot use the scan, you can still use the information contained in it.

NEWSPAPERS

Newspapers can offer a wealth of information about your ancestors. Obituaries are the most fruitful, and usually list a date, place, and cause of death, in addition to names of family members and where they lived. Many list funeral guests from out-of-town, providing broader information about your ancestor's social circles.

"Social notes" can be a source of fascination for modern-day readers. It may seem absurd for a paper to publish "news" such as, "Mrs. Allen Richards hosted an afternoon of cards on Tuesday, attended by Miss Sarah Bell, Mrs. James Banks and Mrs. Steve Timms." But further reflection reminds us that social media networks did not exist years ago, and surely more mundane matters are shared daily on Facebook.

These social reports offer a rich history and cultural context for life in your ancestor's community. You can learn about their hobbies, religious affiliations, travel, hospital visits, military service, celebrations, and more.

Newspapers.com is an incredible source of ancestral newspaper content, and even integrates with Ancestry.com.

> Tip: Use spelling variations when searching for names, and try using first initials. Remember married women used to be known as "Mrs. HisFirstName HisLastName."

FUNERAL/BURIAL RECORDS

I used to focus only on baptisms and skim over burial records, thinking they would not provide much information. I was wrong! Depending on the location and the religion, I have found quite a bit of content about families in their burial records.

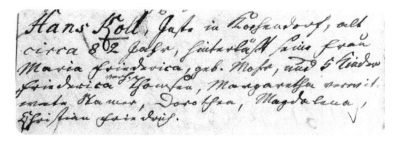

Figure 37: Example burial record

This burial record lists all the children of Hans Koll, as well as his wife's maiden name. So handy.

CENSUS RECORDS

There are entire stories buried deep in census data if you sit down and really study it. I include every census record I can find in my books, and I talk through the various data points in my prose.

Maybe one family owned a radio set in 1940. One person immigrated in 1884. Another person spoke English but could not write it. A man was out of work for half the year. One family lived in a mortgaged farm in 1900, but owned it by

1930, and it was worth $300. Another woman had 7 living children – where is the 7th one? Perhaps a husband had become a naturalized citizen in the last 10 years. Each of these facts has a story in it.

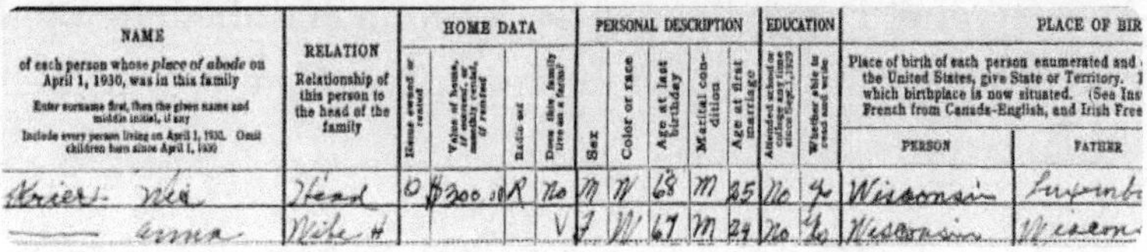

Figure 38: Sample U.S. census record

The one thing to keep in mind is that census data is notoriously unreliable. You will find people whose alleged ability to speak English waxed and waned over the years or whose age or immigration year jumped around. Sometimes if the census-taker had visited several times with no one home, they would turn to a neighbor to answer questions about the family. Oh, the mistakes that come up then!

So take everything with a grain of salt when writing biographies, and simply report what the record says, without claims to its accuracy. For example, "In the 1930 U.S. Census, the census-taker reported that everyone in the family spoke English, but only the children could write it."

IMMIGRATION RECORDS

If you haven't found your immigrant ancestor by typing their name into a database, don't despair. First, make sure to try many different variants of their name (e.g., other spellings or alternate transliterations from non-Cyrillic alphabets). Search for siblings, spouses, and children, in case the transcriber accidentally missed your ancestor's name.

If that does not work, seek other records that may list a year of immigration – the United States census of 1900 is a great place to start (although remember that answers may be inaccurate). This information can inform a search for their naturalization records, which often contain a month, year, and port of origin.

Then comes the really tedious part – you can visually skim through passenger departure or arrival manifests for that time period and cross your fingers. FamilySearch.org and Ancestry.com both have extensive manifest databases.

NON-INDEXED RECORDS ON FAMILYSEARCH

Only a small percentage of the records on FamilySearch.org have been indexed (meaning that the scanned content has been transcribed into searchable text). This means there are often treasures to be found with a little patience and effort.

1. Start by searching the *Catalog* by *Place*.

Figure 39: FamilySearch Catalog

2. Begin typing in the state, county, or town you are looking for.

3. Select the autocompleted entry and hit *Search*.

4. Explore the categorized results. Here I found an "Old Settler's Club" document that I had never seen before.

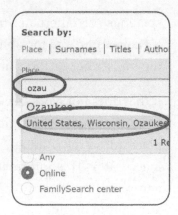

Figure 40: Search by Place

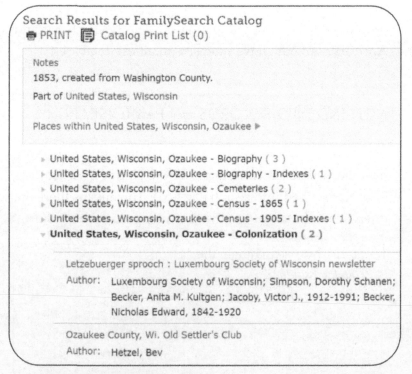

Search Results for FamilySearch Catalog
🖶 PRINT 📋 Catalog Print List (0)

Notes
1853, created from Washington County.
Part of United States, Wisconsin

Places within United States, Wisconsin, Ozaukee ▶

▸ United States, Wisconsin, Ozaukee - Biography (3)
▸ United States, Wisconsin, Ozaukee - Biography - Indexes (1)
▸ United States, Wisconsin, Ozaukee - Cemeteries (2)
▸ United States, Wisconsin, Ozaukee - Census - 1865 (1)
▸ United States, Wisconsin, Ozaukee - Census - 1905 - Indexes (1)
▾ **United States, Wisconsin, Ozaukee - Colonization (2)**

    Letzebuerger sprooch : Luxembourg Society of Wisconsin newsletter
    Author: Luxembourg Society of Wisconsin; Simpson, Dorothy Schanen;
                Becker, Anita M. Kultgen; Jacoby, Victor J., 1912-1991; Becker,
                Nicholas Edward, 1842-1920

    Ozaukee County, Wi. Old Settler's Club
    Author: Hetzel, Bev

Figure 41: FS Catalog search results

5. Click on the link to open the record in FamilySearch.

Figure 42: FamilySearch record

6. Make note of the Item number under "Film," then click the little camera icon under "Format" to see the actual scans. If there is a key symbol over the camera, you may need to visit an authorized Family History Center in person in order to view this record.

7. Don't be confused if you open the camera icon link and see something completely unrelated at first. Many documents are scanned in the same roll of microfilm – this is why you jotted down the Item number. Scroll

down to find a black slide with the correct Item number (there will be one noting the beginning of your section and one noting the end).

Figure 43: Example FS Item section

8. Double-click on a page to see the full content. Here we have a list of original settlers of my ancestral county with year of settlement and year of birth.

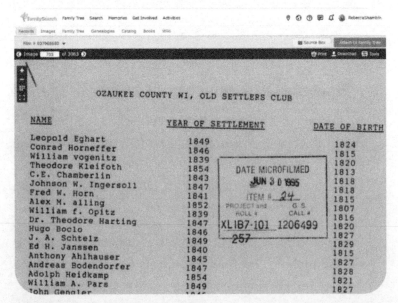

Figure 44: Example FS individual image

This content has an extremely narrow audience, so FamilySearch has not devoted resources to transcribing it. It would never appear in a record search if you typed in "Leopold Eghart," for example. But you can see it would be extremely valuable for someone trying to find his year of immigration.

This document was only three pages long, so it didn't take long to search it manually for my family names. But when I search non-indexed Luxembourg census records for my ancestors, there can be hundreds of slides to wade through, one at a time. I usually have my favorite TV shows on in the background. It is very tedious work, but we genealogists are no strangers to tedium. And the rewards are remarkable.

> Tip: Some documents do have handwritten internal indices that can help narrow down your search. For example, in Luxembourg we have the "Tables Decennales," which man-ually index information in 10-year incre-ments. They are still not searchable by text, but they are incredible finding aids.

INTERVIEWS

If you are lucky enough to have living relatives with ancestors in your book, try to arrange an interview if at all possible. Video recording is best, but audio is very valuable as well. You don't need fancy equipment or microphones – a smartphone or a cassette tape recorder will do. Video chat and even telephone works if they live far away.

Prepare your questions ahead of time and organize them by theme so you can easily pivot if the conversation naturally veers off. Focus on open-ended questions ("How did you ... What kind of ...") rather than yes/no questions ("Did you ever ..."). Assure the person that you are genuinely interested in their story. Most people will demur and insist that their life is nothing special, so you will need to draw them out.

Having direct quotes in your book is a great way to visually break up the blocks of text. You can use pull quotes (the ones bounded by blue lines in this example, with quotes "pulled" out from the main text) to create space and interest. This is especially helpful if you have had trouble sourcing images and documents for a particular chapter.

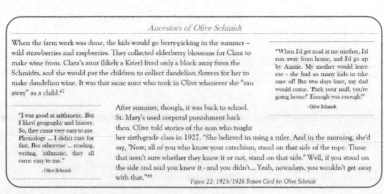

Figure 45: Example interview content in books

PHASE 2: RESEARCH

I used Scribie.com to have my videos transcribed because the thought of typing everything out was too much for me. I had many hours of video and audio content so there was too much to listen to/watch myself without a way to search for keywords. I preferred to spend that time writing.

EXAMPLE INTERVIEW QUESTIONS

- What do you remember about your parents?
- What role did your grandparents play in your life?
- What kind of food did you eat back then?
- How did you celebrate holidays? Do you remember any special gifts?
- What kinds of games did you play?
- What kind of toys did you have?
- What chores were your responsibility?
- What would happen if you misbehaved as a child?
- What were your favorite/least-favorite school subjects?
- How did you get along with your siblings?
- What kind of clothing did you wear? How many pairs of shoes did you have?
- Did anyone in the family ever have a serious illness or injury? What was it like?
- Do you remember any bad storms or winters?
- How did war or economic depression affect you?
- How did you meet your spouse?
- What kind of jobs did you have as an adult?
- What was it like when your children were born?

SHOULD OTHER FAMILY ATTEND INTERVIEWS?

There is not one specific rule of thumb for whether to have other family members present during your interview. Sometimes, having a spouse or child there to guide your interviewee can be invaluable. They know most of this person's "stories" and can prompt them at appropriate moments ("Oh Mom, didn't you say you had scarlet fever that one time?").

On the other hand, shy interviewees may open up more if their spouse is not around. Certainly, if you want to ask them about any "wild times" they had before meeting their spouse, they may be rather reluctant to speak with their current spouse standing right there.

Figure 46: My interview with my great-grandmother, absolutely priceless now that she is gone

You will need to evaluate your subject before deciding which path to take. In my experience, having other family members around to jog memories has been extremely helpful, especially in cases where my subject has challenges with their memory.

PHASE 3:
WRITING

3

You finally have the resources you need to start actually writing your book. Congratulations! Here comes the really fun part … putting it all together.

If you are writing your book from scratch, without FBC, you can jump right in by skipping ahead to page 111.

However, sitting down to write a book can feel very intimidating. Staring at a blank screen can be such a mental roadblock that some people give up before they start.

This is where using FBC can be a wonderful launching point. You can either keep the manuscript that FBC produces as is, or use it as a foundation to build on. After all, tweaking and editing a draft can feel much less overwhelming than writing one from scratch.

You might also take my path, which is using FBC to create the structure of the book, along with charts, summaries, and indexes, but writing your own narrative biographies to be woven in with the rest.

Whichever path you choose, you can start with FBC, using the settings you decided on in the previous section.

USING FAMILY BOOK CREATOR

In this chapter, I will show you the default settings for FBC, as well as the changes I make in my own books. One of the best qualities of FBC is the many ways you can customize it, so please do not take this chapter as the One True Way of Family Books. This is simply an example of how I created my own book. Please download the free official FBC User Guide on www.familybookcreator.com for details and many other options to explore.

LAUNCHING FBC

To open FBC, you must first open a family tree file in FTM. Go to the **Tools** menu, then select *Plugins → Export With Plugin → Family Book Creator*.

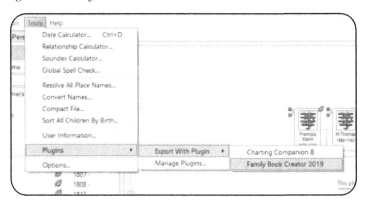

Figure 47: Opening FBC

FBC SECTIONS

FBC has three main workspaces: *Book Items*, *Preferences*, and *About*.

Book Items is where you will choose the people, facts, and media that will appear in your book, as well as front and back matter items, such as an introduction.

Figure 48: FBC Sections

Preferences is where you will tell FBC what styles to use while it is creating your book.

About is where you will enter your personal information and register your copy of FBC.

BOOK ITEMS

MAIN PART

Go to the *Book Items* workspace, and then the **Main Part** tab to begin choosing elements for your book.

When you first launch FBC, it will be loaded with default settings for your book. Before changing anything, you should create a test book and evaluate the results. Under **Main Part**, see the first tab, **Individuals to Include**.

PHASE 3: WRITING

Choose the type of book you are creating (e.g., "Descendants of") and your root person. For this test book, set the *Generations* to be from 0 to 1. Then click *Create Document*. FBC will ask you where to save the document it creates, then take a minute or two to produce it.

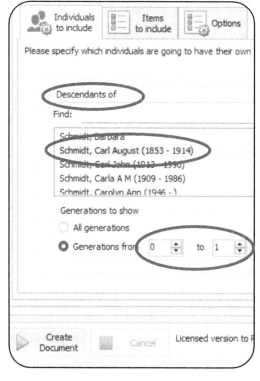

Figure 49: Individuals to Include

Take a look at the resulting document and note any overall structural changes you'd like to make. For example, you might decide to change the font, page size, margins, front matter, citations, included fact types, the photo album, or the indexes. Creating this test book will help you understand how FBC works so you can make those choices.

After your test book, you can return to FBC and start customizing your settings. Continue to make test books periodically as you make additional changes.

Again, this book illustrates some of the most common settings and options, but there are many other choices you can make. **If anything feels too overwhelming, just keep the default settings.**

WHAT IS A FAMILY SECTION?

In terms of FBC, a family section consists of a family chart, a description of the primary person (plus their spouse and children), and an optional photo album for the family.

INDIVIDUALS TO INCLUDE

Because basic information for children is already included in their parents' family section, you may want to skip creating additional family sections for them unless they have a spouse or children (which would be the only new information to share). This is the default setting in FBC and the one I use, but you can choose to create family sections for all children if you desire.

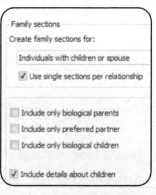

Figure 50: Include details about children

By default, FBC includes adoptive and step-parent relationships, and it includes all partners.

You may want to experiment with the option to "Include details about children." Unselecting it will lead FBC to simply list first names of the couple's children in a single sentence. Selecting it will produce separate mini-sections for each child, listing their birth, marriage, and death information, along with that of their spouse.

Details about children can increase or decrease the length of your book considerably (I did not include them in my first book, but I did add them in my second).

ITEMS TO INCLUDE

Next, choose what will appear in your book, and how.

FAMILY CHART

In the *Family Chart* tab, I like to add person identifiers (unique numbers within this book) and color-coding to the default chart options.

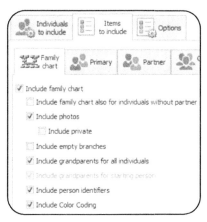

Figure 51: Family Charts

PRIMARY

In the *Primary* tab you can select which fact types to include for the primary person in the chapter. Then for each fact type, you can customize how FBC includes it, as follows:

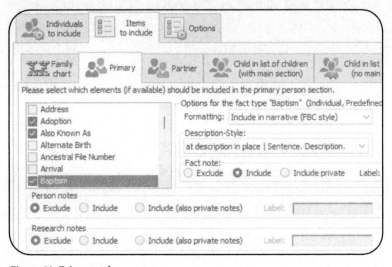

Figure 52: Primary tab

FORMATTING

Two popular ways that FBC can format facts are "Include in narrative (FBC style)" and "Include in list of facts and events." By default, most selected fact types are included in a narrative format (with FBC taking the fact details from FTM and converting them to sentence form).

However, the *Residence* fact type defaults to the list of facts and events. This avoids very repetitive sentences in your book. You can see the difference in the following example.

PHASE 3: WRITING

Charles Peter William reached 62 years of age and died in Port Washington, Ozaukee County, Wisconsin, USA, on February 24, 1949.[3, 26, 27, 29] He passed away at St. Alphonsus Hospital after a short illness. He was buried at St. Mary's Cemetary in Port Washington after February 24, 1949.[26, 27, 29]

More facts and events for Charles Peter William Schmidt:

Residence: 1900	Mequon, Ozaukee County, Wisconsin, USA[34] 13 Age: 13; Farm Laborer Occupation: Farm Laborer; AbleToSpeakEnglish: Yes; AttendedSchool: 10; CanRead: Yes; CanWrite: Yes; EnumerationDistrict: 0017; Single MaritalStatus: Single; Laborer RelationToHead: Laborer
Residence: June 01, 1905	Mequon, Ozaukee County, Wisconsin, USA[35] Age: 18; RelationToHead: Son
Residence: 1910	Ward 3, Port Washington, Ozaukee County, Wisconsin, USA[19]

Figure 53: Fact formatting

In this case, FBC composes sentences about Charles' life and death, but lists his residences in table form.

You can take time to personalize these settings, or you can keep the default options. Because I like to write my own biographies, I have unchecked all but *Birth*, *Marriage*, and *Death* in this section. **For most people, though, this ability for FBC to tell your stories for you is its true superpower.**

DESCRIPTION STYLES

In order to wield this superpower properly, you must understand description styles, which are the rules FBC uses to compose sentences from your facts.

For an in-depth exploration of various description styles, please see the official FBC User Guide. It can be well worth your time to sit down with this section early in the process and try out the various options, so you can set things up in

FTM in a way that produces the sentences you prefer. This feature can seem complex at first, but it is worth the investment of your time and effort to master.

It is important to be consistent in how you enter facts within FTM, especially in the Description field. You may want to select slightly different description styles for various fact types, or even use slightly different description styles for primary people *vs.* their family members.

The *Description-Style* dropdown in the *Primary* tab determines how FBC constructs its sentences, which can have varied results depending on how you use FTM. For example, the default option for the *Baptism* fact is "at *description* in *place*." If you use the Description field in FTM to note the name of a church, this will be perfect for you; but because I use the Description field to list godparents and priests, this style does not work for me.

Here is how my baptism fact looks in FTM:

Figure 54: Baptism fact in FTM

88

So here is how FBC writes about it using default settings:

> Clara Katherine was baptized at Godparents were Fred Jehle and Maria Catherine Krier. The priest was Father Nicolaus in Holy Cross Church, Milwaukee, on January 29, 1888.[5] She received first communion at

Figure 55: Baptism fact from FBC

A better choice for me would be "Sentence. Description." When I properly instruct FBC on my preferred style (by selecting it from the Description-Style dropdown), it produces a more suitable pair of sentences.

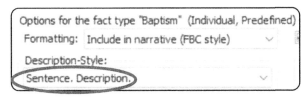

Figure 56: Revised Description-Style

> Clara Katherine was baptized in Holy Cross Church, Milwaukee, on January 29, 1888.[5] Godparents were Fred Jehle and Maria Catherine Krier. The priest was Father Nicolaus. She received first communion at

Figure 57: Revised baptism fact from FBC

Note that "Holy Cross Church" is included in the revised FBC sentence because I added the church name to the place detail of the location in FTM, and then resolved the place name (see page 48).

There is no one correct way to use FTM and FBC to share details about facts. Experiment to discover what feels natural to you, then focus your strategy on that framework. Remember that the more you can customize FBC to compose sentences for you, the less editing you will need to do later.

FACT NOTE

For each fact type, you can choose whether to have FBC include the fact note entered in FTM. This feature can be used in conjunction with the Description field as an alternate way of sharing additional details about a fact.

Figure 58: FBC Fact Type options

PREFERRED AND PRIVATE FACTS

When it comes to preferred vs. alternate facts, FBC has different default options for different fact types. For some facts that legitimately change over time (e.g., occupation), including all versions of the fact makes sense. For others that can only have one true answer, I recommend only including preferred facts otherwise the conflicting facts will all be shared in a confusing way.

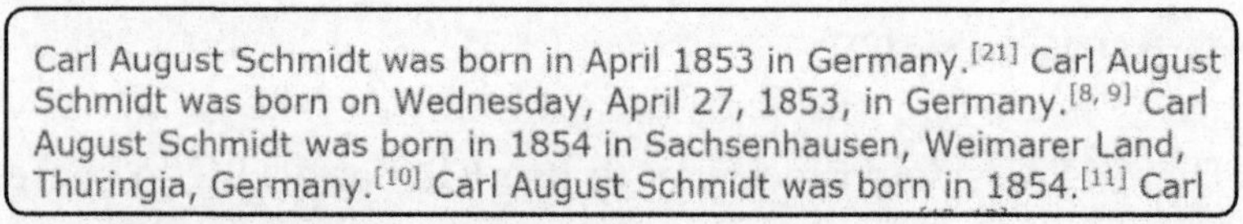

Carl August Schmidt was born in April 1853 in Germany.[21] Carl August Schmidt was born on Wednesday, April 27, 1853, in Germany.[8, 9] Carl August Schmidt was born in 1854 in Sachsenhausen, Weimarer Land, Thuringia, Germany.[10] Carl August Schmidt was born in 1854.[11] Carl

Figure 59: Confusing alternate facts

You can also decide whether to include private facts in your book (disabled by default). Usually facts are private for a reason, so I do not recommend changing this selection.

SOURCE CITATIONS

I always include source citations for all fact types, lending credibility to my work and helping to guide fellow researchers seeking more information.

PERSON AND RESEARCH NOTES

The bottom half of the *Primary* tab lets you choose whether to include Person notes and/or Research notes in your book, as well as portraits.

If you are writing biographies but you don't need them to be heavily formatted or have citations or images, Person Notes is the perfect place to save them. In that case, change the default option from *Exclude* to *Include*.

Many (if not most) people use Research Notes for personal notes to themselves about the progress of their work. In those cases, they should be excluded from the book, which is already the default option.

PARTNER

The options in the *Partner* tab are identical to those of the *Primary* tab, except that they apply to the partner instead and there is a new option to include relationship notes for the couple (selected by default).

Partners have a separate tab to allow you the opportunity to include detailed facts for your primary person but limit details for the rest of the family and thus limit the length of your book.

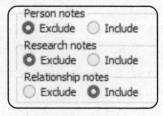

Figure 60: Relationship notes

CHILD IN LIST OF CHILDREN

You can make the same choices for children of the primary person, differentiating how much is included for children with their own family section (chosen in *Individuals to Include* on page 84), and children without.

For children without a main section, you have the option to add spouse or partner details (they are not selected by default, but I did include them in my second book).

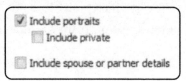

Figure 61: Include spouse or partner details

PHOTO ALBUM

Finally, we come to the photo album. By default, FBC includes all media items attached to the couple in FTM, fitting two to a row, with captions drawn from FTM. Depending on your page size and orientation, the number of rows may vary.

PHASE 3: WRITING

Descendants of Olive Schmidt and Lawrence Watry

Figure 17: 2004-02-09 SCHMIDT sisters - Olive, Ann, Clarice - from Joanne WATRY 2021

Figure 18: 1960-08 SCHMIDT Olive, Joanne and Lawrence WATRY

Figure 19: 1968-01 SCHMIDT, Olive and Lawrence WATRY with Shelly and Mike BLEY

Figure 20: 1990s SCHMIDT, Olive and WATRY, Lawrence

Figure 62: Example FBC Photo Album

Most images will print by default, except for private ones, but you can unselect various options as desired.

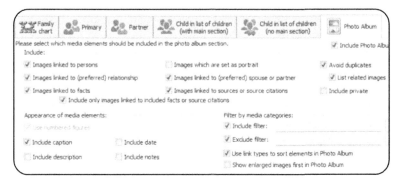

Figure 63: FBC Photo Album Options

If you don't see photos for your primary person's partner, make sure you have selected *Images linked to (preferred) spouse or partner*. If you would like to display portraits but not documents, you can unselect *Images linked to sources or source citations*. Selecting *Avoid duplicates* is key if you have marriage or family photos that are attached to more than one family member.

Private photos are excluded by default, but you may choose to include them if your book is just for you or close family members, or if the photo is private only to prevent it from appearing in your online tree.

The recommended way to control the order of media items in your photo album is to use the *Date* field in FTM. This way FBC will automatically sort your photos chronologically.

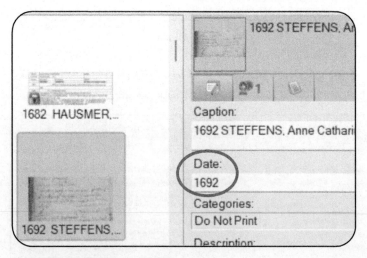

Figure 64: Date field for media items

Alternatively, you can manually re-order your media items in FTM. This can be done using drag and drop or by using the *Move Media Forward/Backward* arrow buttons.

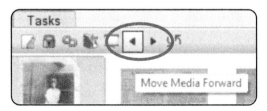

Figure 65: Re-order media in FTM

In the absence of a manual sort from FTM, FBC will sort media items according to the following hierarchy:

1. Type of media
    a. Pictures linked to people
    b. Pictures linked to facts
    c. Pictures linked to relationships
    d. Pictures linked to sources/citations
2. By date, if the media date field has a valid entry
3. Alphabetically by caption
4. Alphabetically by filename

Discussion of media filters can be found on page 118.

Because I prefer to embed images in my narrative biographies, I do not make use of FBC's ability to include photos, but it is very helpful for many people.

OPTIONS

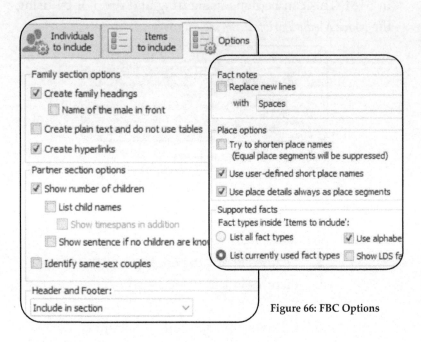

Figure 66: FBC Options

After choosing *who* is in your book, and *what* will be written about them, you can make some decisions about the book overall in the **Options** tab.

I leave most of these settings on their default value. One item I change is that I unselect "Try to shorten place name"; instead, I select "Use user-defined short place names".

> Tip: If you used the "shortened place names" feature back when you were cleaning up your data (page 52), this is where it is relevant, so make sure you have checked this box.

TITLE PAGE

I usually leave the rest of the tabs in the *Book Items* workspace for the end of my process. You can unselect their "include" checkboxes to save processing time when creating your test books.

When you are ready, you can start with the title page.

Figure 67: FBC Title page

I like a lot of white space, so I include only the title of the book, the sub-title, and my name.

COLOPHON

The colophon is also known as the Copyright page. Here is where you can include the year of publication, your name, your location, your email, and your website if you have one.

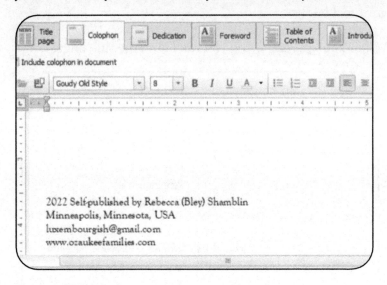

Figure 68: FBC Colophon

This is an important way for readers to track you down if they have questions or further information (or photos) to share with you.

DEDICATION

On the dedication page, you can acknowledge a person you wish to dedicate your research to. You can even add images here if you like.

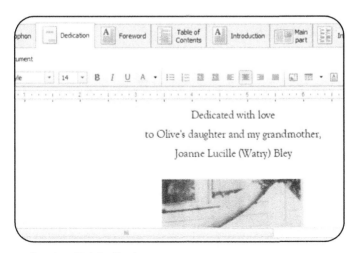

Figure 69: FBC Dedication

FOREWORD

A foreword is generally a section written by someone other than the author of a book. I like to use this area for an epigraph (quote) and a preface, where I write about what inspired me to write the book and how important it is for genealogists to share their work with the world.

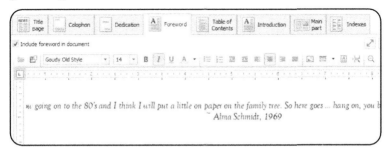

Figure 70: FBC Foreword

TABLE OF CONTENTS

This is an easy one – just check the boxes to include a table of contents in your book.

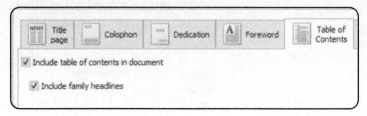

Figure 71: FBC Table of Contents

INTRODUCTION

Next we have the introduction to the book. Here you can explain the structure of the book and what the reader will find in it. I generally use FBC's template, but I add details about the scope of the book and how I use portrait images.

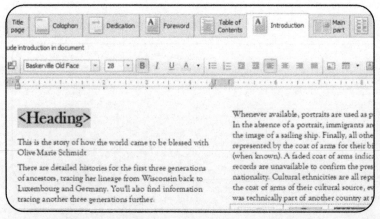

Figure 72: FBC - Introduction

100

PHASE 3: WRITING

At the end of your prose, you can keep the default placeholders, which FBC uses to generate additional content:

- This book presents all known data as of <CurrentDate>.
- <ColorCodingLegend>
- <statistics>

When you run FBC and create the book, these will be replaced with the proper information, helping the reader understand how the colors work and giving some high-level statistics about the tree.

This book presents all known data as of December 31, 2022.

Markings used

Some individuals are marked or tagged by colored dots in family charts. Colored dots are also [s] corresponding names in the index. These markers may help you to see, for example, lineages at shows the meaning of the colored dots.

- Starting person for ancestors (4 colors) of Charles Peter William Schmidt (1886-1949)
- Paternal father's line of Charles Peter William Schmidt (1886-1949)
- Paternal mother's line of Charles Peter William Schmidt (1886-1949)
- Maternal father's line of Charles Peter William Schmidt (1886-1949)
- Maternal mother's line of Charles Peter William Schmidt (1886-1949)
- Starting person for ancestors (4 colors) of Clara Katherine Krier (1888-1974)
- Paternal father's line of Clara Katherine Krier (1888-1974)
- Paternal mother's line of Clara Katherine Krier (1888-1974)
- Maternal father's line of Clara Katherine Krier (1888-1974)
- Maternal mother's line of Clara Katherine Krier (1888-1974)

This document reports the details of 237 individuals, of whom 121 are male and 115 are fema[l] is unknown. Of the 153 individuals with recorded birth and death dates, the average lifespan v males averaged 58 years, and 71 females averaged 64.6 years. The longest living male was Fran[k] 2012), who died aged 93. The longest living female was Bertha Krier (1901-1999), who died

Figure 73: FBC - Generated Introduction

INDEXES

Finally, you can customize the indexes in your book. I do keep the default settings to include a bibliography, but I make several changes to the default settings in the *Index of Places*. I change from "Regular sort order of segments" to "Reverse sort order of segments." This groups nearby locations together in a way that feels more intuitive to me.

Here is what Regular Sort would do:

- Cedar Grove, Ozaukee, Wisconsin, USA
- Cedar Rapids, Linn, Iowa, USA
- Port St. Lucie, St. Lucie, Florida, USA
- Port Washington, Ozaukee, Wisconsin, USA

But if I choose Reverse Sort, I get:

- USA, Florida, St. Lucie, Port St. Lucie
- USA, Iowa, Linn, Cedar Rapids
- USA, Wisconsin, Ozaukee, Cedar Grove
- USA, Wisconsin, Ozaukee, Port Washington

This brings all of my Wisconsin/Ozaukee towns together, which seems more helpful to a reader seeking information about where our ancestors have lived.

I do not use my user-defined place names in the Index, because they can result in visual clutter. I do include a list of each individual reported to have been in that place, using the color-coding dots.

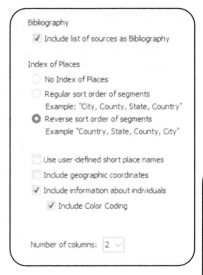

Figure 74: FBC Index of Places

Finally, I prefer two columns for this Index, since I use a landscape orientation. This leaves enough room for most places to exist on one line, without spilling over into the next.

Figure 75: FBC Index of Individuals

I keep most of the default settings for the *Index of Individuals*, except that I add color coding and change from two columns to three.

If you are using portrait orientation for your book, or a smaller page size, you will likely want to keep the default number of columns. You can also change this option in Word after your book has been created (see page 195).

PREFERENCES

GENERAL

The first tab for the **Preferences** workspace (found below **Book Items**) is **General**, and it has multiple sections.

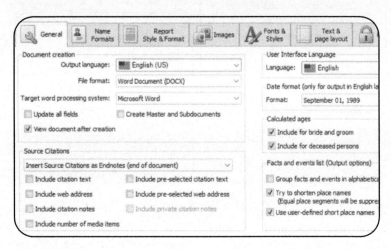

Figure 76: FBC Preferences - General

DOCUMENT CREATION

If you plan to edit the results at all, you should make sure to choose Word Document rather than PDF for the file format.

I recommend that you uncheck *Update all fields*. That feature can slow down FBC quite a bit and you don't need updated fields while you are experimenting. You can always update the fields yourself in Word later (see page 191).

SOURCE CITATIONS

I prefer source citations as endnotes, rather than taking up space at the bottom of each page in the form of footnotes. When FBC runs, it can combine all of the citations from your narrative biographies with its own, and create one single section of them.

If you are concerned about your book being too long, consider excluding text, notes, and/or web addresses from your citations to save space.

I leave all other **General** options on their default settings.

NAME FORMATS

I make only one change in this tab. Under *Family Charts*, I change the format to "First M. Lastname Suffix." The default choice, of "All Given Names Lastname" produced very long names that took up too much space in my charts.

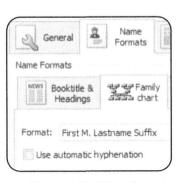

Figure 77: FBC Name Formats

Tip: Take note of this option if you use landscape orientation and have large families in your book (with many children). You will need to minimize chart height.

REPORT STYLE & FORMAT

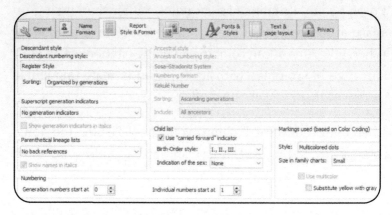

Figure 78: FBC Report Style & Format

Again, I largely keep default settings, but I do remove the "Indication of Sex" under *Child list*, as this is sometimes not specified in documents and I do not like to make assumptions. I also do not select "Substitute yellow with gray" under *Markings Used*.

IMAGES

In this tab, I remove the rounded corners feature from all images. This may seem strange, since I do like rounded corners in my books. But due to limitations in Word, FBC can only create the appearance of rounded corners by adding "invisible" white edging to the image corners. When using a colored or image page background in Word, this shortcut fails. So I round my corners in Word instead (see page 169).

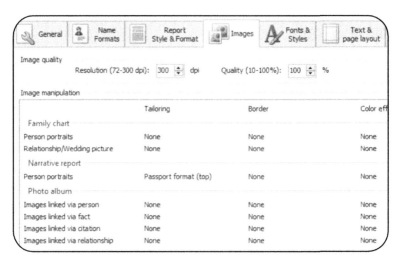

Figure 79: FBC Images

FONT & STYLES

This tab is entirely subject to personal preferences. The default font is Verdana, but I prefer Goudy Old Style. Make sure to match the footnote/endnote font here with the citation font in your narratives, if you are writing any.

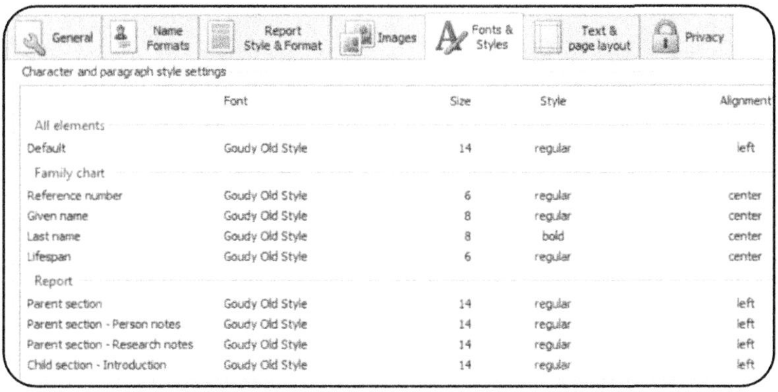

Figure 80: FBC Fonts & Styles

TEXT & PAGE LAYOUT

PAGE LAYOUT

These settings are very particular to my book formatting, meaning they are not necessarily right for you. Create test books and experiment until you like the results.

I like to decrease the default bottom margin, but increase left and right margins. I also increase the header and footer distance to edge. I add a half-inch gutter as well. Importantly, I unselect mirror margins (see page 30).

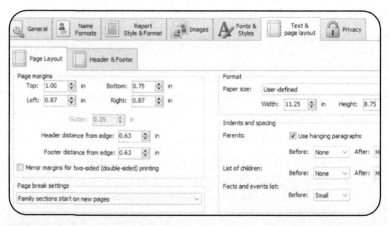

Figure 81: FBC Text & Page Layout

I tell FBC to start my family sections on new pages. I also add bleed to my *Paper Size*, but do not adjust *Indents and Spacing*.

All of these layout elements must match the layout elements in any narrative biographies you want to include.

HEADERS & FOOTERS

Since FBC's default settings include mirror margins, this section does allow you to specify different options for odd and even pages. If you are writing narratives and turned off the mirror margins in FBC, you will only be able to choose a single header and single footer for all pages.

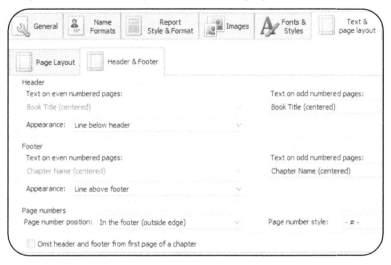

Figure 82: FBC Headers & Footers

FBC automatically changes your default settings here according to your mirror margin choice. It puts the title of the book in the header, and the chapter titles in the footer (along with the page number).

If you would like to customize headers and footers for odd/even pages, you will need to do so in Word after running FBC for the final time.

PRIVACY

FBC does not automatically hide information for living individuals and neither do I, since my book focused on ancestors rather than recent descendants.

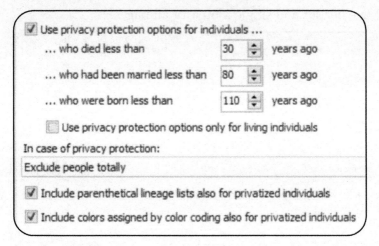

Figure 83: FBC Privacy

You can turn on this feature and adjust privacy settings to your liking. Remember to consider your audience. Who will see this book? Just your siblings or children? Distant cousins? Anyone who orders a copy from your website? Each choice has different implications for privacy concerns.

SAVING SETTINGS

Now that you have spent all this time choosing settings, you may find you prefer different options for different types of books (for example, ancestor *vs.* descendant), different lengths of books, or even different branches of your family. Or maybe you would just like to experiment without risking all of the selections you have already settled on. Fortunately, FBC has a way of saving settings and then reloading them.

To do this, go to the **Preferences** workspace, and look below the tab sections. Click *Save Settings* to save your current choices (remember to use a descriptive filename so you can remember what kind of settings these are). Later on, you can re-use these settings by clicking *Load Settings* and navigating to that file you saved. At any time, you can click *Reset Settings* and revert FBC back to its default options.

Figure 84: FBC Save/Load/Reset Settings

INCLUDING BIOGRAPHIES WITH FBC

If you are writing narrative biographies and plan to use FBC, you will have two options for where to save them to be incorporated into your final book.

INCLUDING BIOGRAPHIES IN NOTES (FBC)

There is a basic method you can use to create narrative books with FBC. This consists of writing your biographies in the *Notes* section of a person (or fact) in FTM and then directing FBC to include the photo album at the end of each couple's section. This is the simplest, most straightforward way to include biographies in your book.

Many people opt for this method, and you should certainly consider if it works for you. You will likely finish your book much more quickly this way.

I started with this method but quickly abandoned it for the following reasons:

1. I wanted more formatting control over my biographies than I could achieve in *Notes*.
2. I wanted to include my photos and documents within the biographies, rather than at the end.
3. I wanted to control the size and crop of my photos and documents precisely.
4. I wanted to include citations in my biographies.
5. I wanted to be able to have my biography content included in the *Index of Individuals*.

Above all, visual layout is extremely important to me. I wanted this to look like a "real" book as much as possible. So, I decided to skip "simple" and invest a little more time and effort.

INCLUDING BIOGRAPHIES VIA WORD

Microsoft Word offers all of the formatting, indexing, and citation features that I was looking for in writing narratives, and luckily FBC offers a way to integrate it via FTM.

Using Word, I write one illustrated biography for each couple in the first three generations of my book (each in their own separate .docx file). Then FBC is able to incorporate those files when it runs, smoothly blending indexing, markup, and citations with the rest of the hard data. Magic!

ATTACHING BIOGRAPHIES (FTM)

Attaching your Word documents to people in FTM is as simple as attaching photos to them. The simplest way is to drag and drop the file from Explorer into the person's *Media* tab in the **Person** workspace in FTM.

Alternatively, you can click *New* from the person's *Media* tab and navigate to your file to insert it directly.

Figure 85: Media Tab in FTM

You can mark these files as "Private" if you do not wish for them to synchronize to your public Ancestry.com tree. Privacy is indicated by the lock symbol at the bottom left corner of the icon, as seen in the "Notes" file here.

Close the biography file in Word after attaching it in FTM, to avoid accidentally making edits to an old version of the file. This is very important. When you need to make edits later, double-click the file from within FTM to open it in Word, or find it in the appropriate FTM media folder on your computer's hard drive.

> Tip: If at any point after you run FBC, you notice that the most recent changes to your narrative biography are not appearing, check to see if you have been editing an old file, rather than the version that is attached to the person in FTM.

ADDING FBC MEDIA CATEGORIES (FTM)

Simply attaching the file in FTM is not enough. You need to give FBC instructions about how to use it, by assigning Media Categories to the file in FTM. You will find the most up-to-date list of categories in the official User Guide for FBC, as well as in the FBC User Group on Facebook. They are not built in to FTM, so you must add them the first time you use them.

To assign categories to a media item in FTM, right-click on it in the **Media** workspace and select *Categorize Media.*

To add a new category that doesn't exist yet (like the FBC categories), click *Add.*

Figure 86: Categorize Media

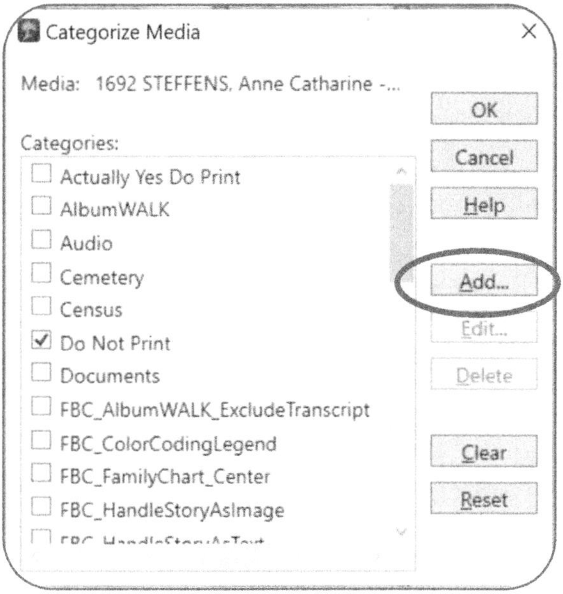

Figure 87: Add new category

Type in a new category name and click *OK.*

Figure 88: New category name

Now watch out! Before you do anything else, note that your new category has not been assigned to this particular item yet. **You must select it specifically**.

Figure 89: New category not added yet

Only then can you click *OK* to close the *Categorize Media* window.

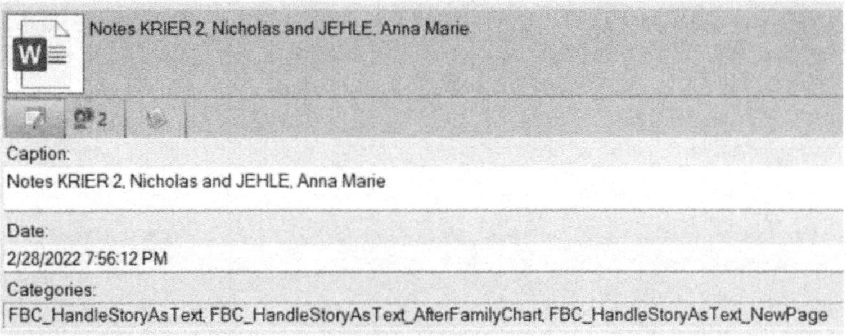

	Notes KRIER 2, Nicholas and JEHLE, Anna Marie

Caption:
Notes KRIER 2, Nicholas and JEHLE, Anna Marie

Date:
2/28/2022 7:56:12 PM

Categories:
FBC_HandleStoryAsText, FBC_HandleStoryAsText_AfterFamilyChart, FBC_HandleStoryAsText_NewPage

Figure 90: FBC Media Categories

Here are the categories that I use:

FBC_HandleStoryAsText tells FBC that you want this content to be inserted in your book – this is critical!

FBC_HandleStoryAsText_AfterFamilyChart tells FBC you want this content inserted after the family chart (optional).

FBC_HandleStoryAsText_NewPage tells FBC you want the content to start on a fresh page, not inserted directly under the family chart (optional).

There are many other categories you can explore.

INCLUDING MEDIA ITEMS (FBC)

When you are ready to run FBC, go to **Book Items → Main Part** → *Items to Include* → *Photo Album*. Make sure you have checked *Include Photo Album* or your narrative biographies will not appear in your book.

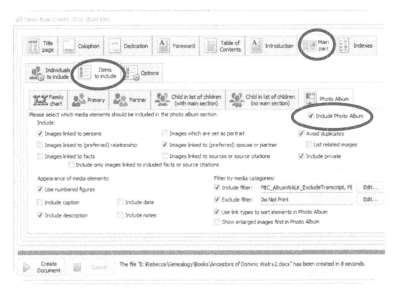

Figure 91: FBC Photo Album

For the most part, I do not use FBC's automatic inclusion of photos at the end of each person's section, because I prefer to have control over when and where they are displayed in my biographies. So, you might think I would not include a Photo Album here. However, this would more aptly be named "Media Album" since it also includes the *documents* you have attached in your tree.

FILTERING MEDIA ITEMS (FBC)

If you want FBC to include both your biographies *and* every image attached to your ancestors in FTM, you can stop here. FBC will naturally do this.

However, if you want to include *only* your biographies and *not* solo images, you need to use FBC filters.

You might assume that all you need to do is add your biographies to the *Include* filter and you are done, because that is all you want to include. *This will not work.*

> Tip: All images are included by default when you enable the Photo Album. If you do not want an image in your book, you need to specifically exclude it.

If you do not wish for any individual photos to appear in your FBC book, you must create some sort of "Do Not Print" media category in FTM and apply it to **every** photo that is attached to the people in your book. For simplicity, I apply it to every photo in my FTM library as a whole.

After you have applied this media category in FTM, you can open FBC and Exclude your "Do Not Print" category from the photo album in your book.

When *would* you use the Include filter? Only as an override to the Exclude filter.

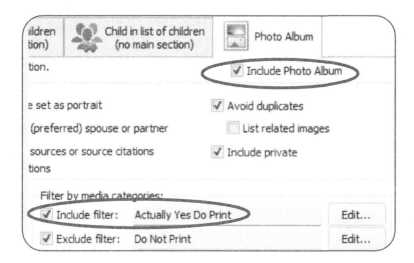

Figure 92: FBC media category filters

For example, there are a few documents attached to my fourth and final generation in the book that I actually did want to print. I had not written narrative biographies for that generation so I thought the documents would be a nice addition. Therefore I created a category called "Actually Yes Do Print" and added it to those media items in FTM, and to the Include filter in FBC.

Even though they would normally have been excluded via their category of "Do Not Print," the Include filter saved them, and they appeared in my book.

Could I have just left them with no category at all and had the same results? Yes, but this way in the future I can blindly categorize every photo in my FTM library with "Do Not

119

Print" without having to worry about skipping those few items every time.

If you get confused, just remember that *Include* does nothing if you have not *Excluded* already.

TESTING BIOGRAPHIES (FBC)

After you have created at least a draft of your first biography chapter, attach it in FTM and do an FBC test run for that generation only.

Make sure your margins are where you want them and that everything looks smooth before you go any further. Trust me, it is far better to find margin problems now than seven chapters later. Also double-check that your citation fonts are matching up.

Continue testing after you complete each biography, running FBC for all generations and checking over the results. Try to catch any problem as soon as it arises.

> Tip: Make any edits in the individual biography Word documents, not your final compiled book. This ensures the edits will be included when you run FBC again at the end of your writing process or in the future.

PHASE 3: WRITING

USING WORD WITH FBC SUMMARY

1. Create a biography for your couple in Word, composing text (page 125) and incorporating desired images (page 56).

2. Add citations (footnotes or endnotes) (page 147).

3. If desired, add appropriate codes for indexing places and individuals (page 178).

4. Attach biography as a media item in FTM and close the file in Word (page 113).

5. Add FBC media categories to the media item in FTM (page 114).

6. Select relevant FBC settings to include biographies (page 117).

7. Run FBC and evaluate the results (page 120).

8. Open the individual biography document from within FTM and make required edits, then run FBC again. Repeat as needed.

CHAPTER STRUCTURE

Each chapter in my books focuses on the life of one couple and their children (see "What is a Generation?" on page 13). I begin each one with an immediate family chart (including parents and grandparents of the main couple). This helps situate the chapter in the mind of the reader, reminding them of where we are in the larger tree. If you use FBC, it can automatically create these charts for you.

Then I include the narrative biography that I write, which adds context and color to the basic facts. I incorporate images within the text of the narrative biography as I write. This section is optional. If it feels too overwhelming for you, feel free to opt out of the biography and stick with the basics.

Finally, I end each chapter with a recitation of basic genealogical data – birth, marriage, and death information for the family. Some of that data is also embedded in the biography, but I like to have everything collated in one spot for other researchers to reference. FBC also creates this automatically, or you can reference things like "LifeStory" on Ancestry.com.

If you are not creating narrative biographies with images, you will likely want to include a photo album for the couple at the end of each chapter.

I place all of my endnotes at the end of the book, instead of after each chapter (see page 148).

CHAPTER ORDER

Contents

Figure 93: Chapter order

I organize book sections by generation, starting with the most recent. So, my first generation is the parents of my root person, Olive Schmidt. The second generation is her grandparents, and third is her great-grandparents. Within the generations, I work my way "down" the pedigree chart

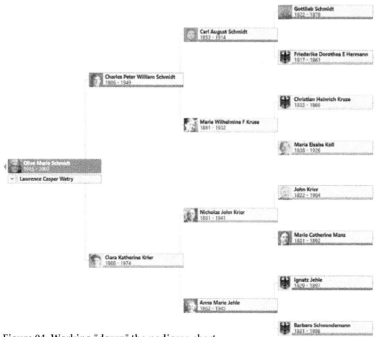

Figure 94: Working "down" the pedigree chart

(starting with the couple at the top of each column, working columns from left to right).

There is no one correct order for couples or generations. You might prefer to follow the entire paternal half of your tree first, and then go back for the maternal half. Whatever you choose, make sure to be consistent throughout your book.

Some researchers like to include separate chapters on geographical areas, such as hometowns or home countries of their ancestors. You can include a short history of the area, demographics, important buildings, and even a modern-day glimpse of the area today. This is also a great space for general community photos, of places like churches or factories. I chose to incorporate this content directly into my biographies, but there are many ways to structure a book.

I add other "bonus content" at the end of the book, like fan charts, maps, and word clouds.

I also include a "Methods" page to explain how I gathered my information and content, and show some strategies in case other researchers would like to follow my work.

Finally, I finish with indexes and citations (bibliography and end notes).

WRITE IN ORDER

With my first book, I jumped around the timeline, writing whichever chapter struck my fancy next. This was ultimately a hassle, because I could never remember what I had already written about historical events that crossed families, such as the Civil War. I ended up having to delete duplicate content in some cases or squeeze in forgotten details in others.

For my second book, I promised myself that I would write the biographies in order. This meant the hardest chapters were first since I had the most content to wade through. It was a bit demoralizing to spend so long on a single chapter early on, but it was heartening that each subsequent generation went faster and faster.

And since layout is so important to me, it was a thousand times easier to include everything properly the first time. Any time I had to go back and insert new content was stressful, because, unless it took up an entire page, it affected the placement of everything after it in that chapter.

For example, I wrote the first four pages in Charles' chapter and arranged all of my images beautifully. But when I went back to insert a paragraph of text to the first page, my beautiful layout was destroyed. I could not just move everything forward because the wedding photos took up an entire page themselves. The only solution was to delete or streamline other text, or shrink my images so everything fit in those first two pages again.

Figure 96: Example biography layout

Figure 95: Example layout after content insertion

Do yourself a favor and write your biographies in order.

WRITING BIOGRAPHIES

My original plan was to stick with tried-and-true genealogical book data like birth, marriage, and death facts. Then I sat down and thought about my intended audience (my grandmother) and decided that seeing only names, dates, and places would not be as interesting to her as it is to me. She would want to read stories and really learn about her ancestors. I needed to add historical facts and context to help her understand our family's emigration and foundation in the United States.

WHAT TO WRITE

Within each chapter, I write chronologically. I start with the birth of each couple, then leap forward to their marriage (see "What is a Generation?" on page 13). After that, I move forward in time, incorporating data, documents, and photographs until their deaths.

When I have a document, I talk about what the document says, what it implies, and what its consequences were. Sometimes I describe photos, but other times they stand on their own. Each piece of evidence gets at least one paragraph. Occasionally, the *lack* of evidence and my efforts to find it are the story I tell.

I structure chapters based on evidence I have. I move from line to line, going down their profile chronologically in FTM.

So, for my section on Marie Catherine Mans, I started with her birth. I was lucky enough to find her family on three Luxembourg censuses, from 1846, 1847, and 1851. Normally those would be in a chapter about her parents, but she was the third generation and her parents were never going to get their own chapter, so I included scans of those records and discussions of the contents. Which of her siblings were still at home? Was anyone abroad?

Birth	23 Jan 1831	Useldange, Redange
Residence	1846	Useldange, Redange
Residence	1847	Useldange, Redange
Residence	1851	Useldange, Redange
Arrival	09 Aug 1852	New York County, New
Residence	1860	Belgium, Ozaukee Cou
Residence	1870	Belgium, Ozaukee Cou
Residence	1880	Belgium, Ozaukee Cou
Death	1892	Lake Church, Belgium,
Death	07 Jul 1892	Sheboygan County, W
Death	17 Jul 1892	Lake Church, Belgium,
Departure		Antwerpen, Antwerpen,
Race		White
PlaceofOri...		Creves
Travel		Ship: Lawrens
Burial		Lake Church, Belgium,
Shared Facts with John Krier		
Marriage	13 Aug 1854	Lake Church, Belgium

Figure 97: Marie Mans FTM data

their own chapter, so I included scans of those records and discussions of the contents. Which of her siblings were still at home? Was anyone abroad?

Then I discussed her family's emigration and her marriage. I included each of the census records I could find for her and her husband's family, as well as some content I found in another researcher's book about the town.

I sprinkled in photos of her home and her other children. I usually include sibling wedding and family portraits when I can find them. Wedding photos in particular tend to include multiple generations and can be very helpful, even if they are only siblings of my direct ancestor. If they were difficult to track down or they provide evidence for the family moving to a new town, I will sometimes include baptism records for the siblings as well.

Finally, I added Marie's death records and a modern photo of her gravestone.

WRITING ABOUT IMMIGRATION

Immigration is one of my favorite topics to write about. Once I find my ancestor on a passenger manifest, I start researching the ship itself, as well as the captain. Sometimes I find photos or paintings of the ship (be careful because multiple ships sometimes share the same name, or one ship might shift through multiple names during its lifetime).

This attention to detail actually helped me confirm that a woman I'd found in a manifest was in fact the one I'd been

Figure 98: Portrait of S. Santelli, who captained the ship my ancestor took to America

looking for. Since she travelled alone, I had nothing but a name and birth year to stand as evidence that it wasn't some other "Anna Jehle." But when I discovered that both her brother and her sister had travelled on the same ship under the same captain in previous years, I felt confident it was her.

Can't find your ancestor on a manifest? You can still research and write about what immigration from their homeland was like during that time. You can include paintings of Ellis Island or talk about the conditions in steerage on a passenger ship. Write about how long the voyage would have been and how your ancestor might have travelled over land after arrival. Muse about what it must have been like to attempt this trip with small children in tow, carrying everything the family owned in a single trunk.

You can even write about how you can't find immigration records. Talk about the various databases and collections you have searched through. Your ancestor's absence from the records is still data worth having. Or perhaps the departure lists from the port they would have used were all burned in a fire, and you can share a little history about that. All of these concepts help place your ancestor in the world and in the mind of the reader.

DIFFICULT SUBJECTS

No genealogist is a stranger to finding "skeletons in the closet." Sometimes we unearth information that does not fit the happy narrative of our book. Only you can decide whether to include sensitive topics in your family history. Sometimes that decision rests on how long ago everything happened. Sometimes it rests on who would be embarrassed if it came to light today.

In my own experience, I have mostly chosen to include everything, but I try to do so with sensitivity. When I had an ancestor who was universally known for his alcohol use, it didn't feel right to leave his defining characteristic out of my book. But I did include some hypotheses about what was behind it (his father and grandfather had both been big drinkers, and he suffered from a painful medical condition that he could have been self-medicating for), as well as quotes from his descendants stating that he never drank at home and was never abusive. He was simply a human, with human flaws.

Babies conceived or born out of wedlock can also be a sensitive topic for some. In most cases, I simply state the facts and move on – "John and Jane married in June of 1910. In November, little William was born." When biological parentage is uncertain, I explain the DNA research I have performed and how confident I feel in the conclusions.

Again, my books have focused on ancestry. Topics like these could have a far greater impact in a descendant book about recent history. Be responsible with what you find and the harm it could inflict on present-day family if revealed. Your books should bring curiosity and joy to the world, not pain.

ADDING CONTEXT

Historical context is key for creating a fully fleshed-out biography. If you don't have as much evidence as you'd like, research the situation and write about what you *do* have and how likely it is that your ancestor might have been a part of it. Did they live through a depression? A war? An epidemic? How might that have affected their lives?

Remember, as researchers, we are constantly steeped in history and context. Your average reader is probably not. Help draw a picture for them, to bring their ancestors to life.

If an interviewee, a newspaper article, or some other document mentions something noteworthy, like having a collapsible bathtub, go hunting for more information. How common was that? How did they fill it? How often would a person bathe back then? Can you find a photo or a drawing of one to include?

Figure 99: Collapsible bathtub

I had trouble visualizing this concept when a person I was interviewing described it, and I assumed my readers would have the same challenge. Finding a photograph was a huge help and added that extra flair to the biography.

None of my direct ancestors are mentioned in stories of "The Great Indian Scare of 1862" in Wisconsin. But it was a significant event that would have affected everyone, so I included it and took time to explore the historical underpinnings. Why were American Indians so feared, and why were settlers so quick to believe an attack was coming? What would that long night have been like for terrified parents? What mix of relief and shame did they feel when they realized it was all a hoax? How might that night have affected their children's future cultural attitudes?

None of those details were required to build my tree, but they helped show what life was really like for my ancestors, and I find that just as important as birth and death dates. These kinds of details are what can turn a simple collection of facts into a story – into a life.

WHAT IS TRUTH?

Be cautious in your claims, especially when working with interviewees. I tried to avoid saying things like, "The family did XYZ" and stuck with "Ralph remembered the family doing XYZ." It's not, "No one in the house could speak English in 1900;" rather, it should be "No one in the house was reported to speak English in the 1900 census."

All you can do is share what you have found and where you found it. After that, you can allow your readers to draw their own conclusions.

This isn't to say you can't share your opinions. I have shared multiple stories with caveats such as, "Considering ABC, this seems doubtful, but one person did claim that XYZ happened." Or "The 1900 census showed no one in the household speaking English, although this was unlikely for the children who had been in school for several years." Or even, "Here is a family legend. We don't have any evidence to support it, but isn't it exciting to imagine?"

EXAMPLE BIOGRAPHY EXCERPTS

These passages from my biographies shed light on some of the ways you can "liven up" what could be seen as a list of dry facts. I did report those facts, but I also added commentary on what they represented or why they might have been the case.

WRITING & RESEARCH PROCESS

In this excerpt, I will walk you through an example of my writing and research process for my great-great-grandparents, Charles and Clara. Although I try to collect as much research as possible in the previous phase, I always end up digging further on something as I start writing.

I began with the family lore that Charles and Clara met while he was working on the railroad. I also knew the church they attended and their marriage date, and I had a wedding photo. Here is what I created from that point on. Layout and citations are no longer present, but I am including the images so you can see some of what I found. Italicized text represents actual excerpts from my book.

I started by researching the local railroad at that time and concluding that it must have been the Milwaukee Northern Railway Interurban line. I researched the company, mostly using Google and the Transit Museum. I was surprised and interested to learn that it was powered electrically, and I assumed my readers would feel the same. I reached out to the archives to ensure I had their permission to include the photos in my book. Then I asked my grandmother's cousin to ask his mother for any more details she could remember.

Figure 100: Milwaukee Northern Railway Interurban car, from interurbantrail.com

In October 1907, The Milwaukee Northern Railway began its inter-urban rail service between Milwaukee and Cedarburg. The next month, they extended service to Port Washington. The interurban was powered electrically, without the smoke and cinders of the railroad. According to his daughter Clarice Schmidt, Charles was living in Thiensville and working on building the line. He walked home every night, but as the rail extended northward, it became too far away to be practical. Like many rail workers, Charles chose to board with a local family – he rented a room from the Kriers. There, he met Clara, and history was made. How many hundreds of us descendants would not exist here today without the Milwaukee Northern Railway?

Figure 101: 1907 Milwaukee Northern construction crew, south of Cedarburg, from The Milwaukee Electric Railway & Transit Historical Society

I was thrilled to find some small photos of railway workers, and paused to think of how amazing it would be if my ancestor was in one of them. We will almost certainly never find out.

Next, I used FamilySearch.org to find a wedding record for Charles and Clara. Church records in that area are not indexed, but I was able to track it down by searching all wedding listings for that year. I also received a baby portrait from my grandmother's cousin.

Figure 102: 1908 Schmidt/Krier wedding record

Charles and Clara married in October of 1908 in Lake Church, witnessed by Oscar and Mathilda Krier (Clara's brother and her cousin).

The young couple moved into a house at 817 Michigan Street (now 523) in Port Washington. Their first child, Carla, was born the following August.

My grandmother's cousin still lives in this county. Using an address from an old postcard, he found the street address of the house and was able to go photograph it for me.

Figure 103: 1908 Charles Schmidt and Clara Krier wedding portrait

Figure 104: 2022 Home of Charles Schmidt and Clara Krier after marriage

Figure 105 c. 1910 Carla Schmidt

By the 1910 census, the family was living in Port Washington, renting a house on West Valley Street. The young couple were 23 and 22 years old, living with 8-month-old Carla. Both adults could reportedly read and write.

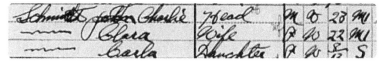

Figure 106: 1910 United States Census - Charles Schmidt household

I didn't know what a "fireman" was when I first read it on the census record. I first assumed it was the modern version, a person who fights fires, but quickly learned otherwise, so I included that explanation in my book. I also took a quote from a memoir written by one of Charles and Clara's sons. The image of the power house was sent to me by another researcher working on this geographical area after I posted a question to that town's Facebook group.

"Charlie" was working as a fireman at the Milwaukee Northern Railway power house. In this circumstance, a "fireman" did not

extinguish fires – rather, he ensured that the fires remained alive and roaring to continue powering the plant and thus the electric railway and streetcars.

Figure 107: Power plant where Charles Schmidt worked as a fireman

His son Ralph remembered visiting the plant as a child: "The generator was run by a great big steam engine and I mean big!" The plant was just south of Smith Brothers Fish Shanty, and Charles' friend Deloise Smith would give him "all the fish he wanted."

The chapter goes on to share more family photos, Charles' WWI draft card, more census records, a school report card, a photo of a player piano, newspaper clippings, a photo of a collapsible bathtub, an ad for a Delco-Light plant, photos of flour sacks designed to serve as sewing fabric during The Depression, postcards, obituaries, and funeral cards. It is officially the longest biography I have written yet, coming in at a whopping 61 pages, plus endnotes!

Adding non-family photos like the piano and the flour sacks helped illustrate stories that I had collected about the family. They were central parts of the family's life back then, but modern-day readers would have little context to understand what was really meant. Even *I* did not have a good sense of them until I started digging and became fascinated.

TELLING A STORY WITH CENSUS DATA

Here is an example of what I did with a census record. You can see why I switched to landscape orientation. It is very difficult to read in detail. I had to chop the image in two here in order to make it remotely legible in portrait orientation.

In my text, you will see a few references to memoirs written by a couple of children in the family (yes, I had access to multiple memoirs and was incredibly grateful for them).

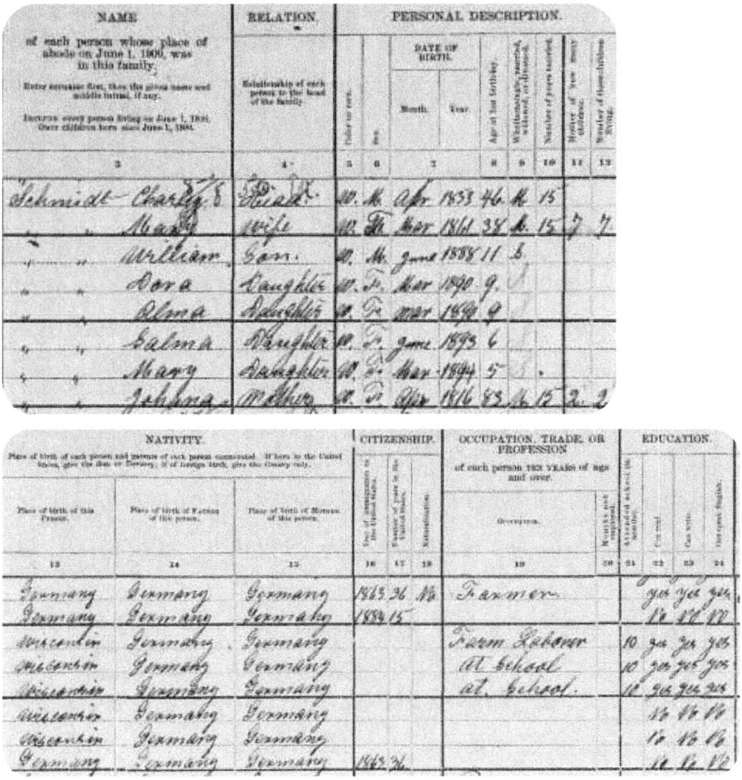

NAME	RELATION	PERSONAL DESCRIPTION								
3	4	5	6	7 (Month)	7 (Year)	8	9	10	11	12
Schmidt Charles	Head	W	M	Apr	1853	46	M	15		
" " Mary	Wife	W	F	Mar	1861	38	M	15	7	7
" " William	Son	W	M	June	1888	11	S			
" " Dora	Daughter	W	F	Mar	1890	9				
" " Alma	Daughter	W	F	Mar	[illegible]	9				
" " Salma	Daughter	W	F	June	1893	6				
" " Mary	Daughter	W	F	Mar	1894	5				
" " Johanna	Mother	W	F	Apr	1816	83	W	15	2	2

NATIVITY			CITIZENSHIP			OCCUPATION, TRADE, OR PROFESSION		EDUCATION			
13	14	15	16	17	18	19	20	21	22	23	24
Germany	Germany	Germany	1865	36	Na	Farmer			yes	yes	yes
Germany	Germany	Germany	1884	15					[illegible]	[illegible]	[illegible]
Wisconsin	Germany	Germany				Farm Laborer		10	yes	yes	yes
Wisconsin	Germany	Germany				At School		10	yes	yes	yes
Wisconsin	Germany	Germany				At School		10	yes	yes	yes
Wisconsin	Germany	Germany							[illegible]	[illegible]	[illegible]
Wisconsin	Germany	Germany							[illegible]	[illegible]	[illegible]
Germany	Germany	Germany	1865	36					[illegible]	[illegible]	[illegible]

Figure 108: 1900 U.S. Census - Carl Schmidt household

When the census-taker visited in 1900, "Charley" (Carl) and Marie were 46 and 38, and owned their farm with a mortgage. Surprisingly, their birthdays, birth places, parents' birthplaces, and even their immigration years were all listed correctly. It was noted that Carl had become a naturalized citizen (unfortunately, naturalization records are frustratingly sparse and it has not been possible to determine which of the many "Carl/Charles Schmidt from Germany" records is his). Carl could read, write, and speak English – but Marie could reportedly do none of these things, even after 15 years in the country.

Marie reported having had only seven children, all of whom were still living. It is a surprising statistic for the time, to not have had any stillbirths or childhood deaths. However, she is clearly not acknowledging her first baby here, so it is possible she merely did not want to share such private information.

William and the twins could apparently read, write, and speak English. At ages 5 and 6, "Salma" and Mary were too young to have attended school and could of course neither read nor write. It is interesting to notice that they also supposedly could not speak English. This correlates with a common local practice of speaking native languages in the home, and only having the children learn English at school. One can imagine their communication struggles in their first weeks. No wonder Dora did not like her first school experiences, as she shared in her memoir.

Carl's stepmother Hanna Acker was the last entry in the household, her husband Gottlieb having passed away back in 1878. This correlates with Alma's childhood memories of her step-grand-

mother living with them. Hanna, too, had apparently never learned to speak English, read, or write, which likely would have been a great challenge when interacting with the world beyond the farm.

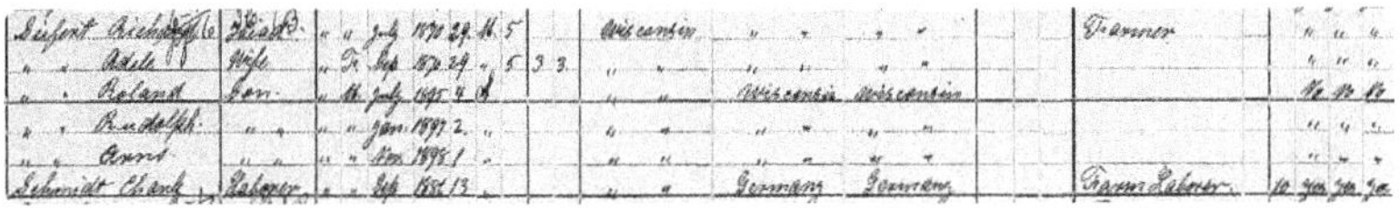

Figure 109: 1900 U.S. Census - Charles Schmidt in Richard Seifert household

Julius and Charles were missing from the Schmidt household in 1900. They were 15 and 13 years old at the time, so they had been hired out to other farms to earn money for the family. Julius was living with the Herman Seifert family as a "laborer," and "Charly" was working for the Richard Seifert family. Carl himself sometimes worked for Seifert farms in the summer, so this placement makes sense. Both boys reported having attended 10 months of school that year, so they likely worked after school and on weekends.

On one level, I am just writing out what the census record says. But I am also pointing out surprising elements or noting how they fit in with other records of the time. I add a little historical context to show whether something is unusual or to be expected back then. And I talk about the implications of the census answers. What would it mean for someone not to speak English in Wisconsin in 1900?

ADDING HISTORICAL CONTEXT

My ancestor Carl was a toll gate operator in 1880 Wisconsin. But what did that mean at that time, in that place? Here is the research I did to try and bring that part of his story to life.

It may be more than you want to do for your book, but I found it fascinating. I had never heard of "plank roads" before. Again, I turned to Google and local historical societies to educate myself and share that new knowledge in my book.

Carl and Sophie moved into the toll gate house between Cedarburg and Thiensville, which stood at the corner of Highway 57 (Cedarburg Road) and Highland Road. The gate controlled northern access to the Milwaukee-Cedarburg Plank Road. Plank roads (or "farmer's highways") were designed to help farmers transport goods and people all year round, even when the weather was bad and the ground was muddy. They were built by laying two parallel timbers at least 18 feet apart (wide enough for two wagons), then laying 3-foot-wide planks across the timbers. The plank roads were built by private companies, not the government, so their maintenance was funded via the collection of tolls.

Built with the best of intentions, plank roads were not without problems, especially weather-related. As the Ozaukee County Historical Society pointed out, "Planks would expand and turn brittle in summer temperatures, leading to surface fractures, and wet winter weather would often rot them after five years of use." Rainy seasons were particularly difficult, as were areas next to natural springs, like the Cedarburg Road crossing. The "road" would quickly become a muddy sinkhole as water and soil seeped up through the planks. Farmers began carrying big log chains with them, to help tow each other out of the mud.

PHASE 3: WRITING

Toll gate operators had quite the responsibility – they had to make sure the gate was attended 24 hours a day. Tolls varied between one and four cents per horse (except on Sundays, when families riding to church were not charged). The "gate" itself was merely a long cedar pole, about six inches in diameter that stretched across the entire road. One end was fastened to a fulcrum with a steel bar, and the other rested on posts on the far side of the road, held down by a basket filled with stones. After payment, the operator would remove the basket and lift the "gate" with a rope.

This photo is one of the only pieces of evidence indicating that the northern toll gate ever existed. The southern one is far better documented. We do not know if Carl and his family are the people in the photograph.

Figure 110 c. 1900 North Mequon Toll Gate, from the Ozaukee County Historical Society

Did any of those details absolutely need to be in a family history book? Probably not. I could have left it as a single line about his occupation. But these details helped me truly imagine what life was like for my ancestor. I can picture him helping farmers out of sinkholes or being dragged out of bed to collect a penny from an early morning customer. And frankly, it was fun to research.

This particular piece of context also helps place the ancestor geographically in the mind of the reader. Now every time they drive through that intersection, they can imagine the giant gate that used to be there and wonder how different a wooden plank road would look and feel to cross.

Having shared this book with dozens of people face-to-face, I can tell you that many of them pause on this page to read and learn more.

SENSITIVE TOPICS

As discussed earlier, babies born to unmarried women can be a sensitive subject for some people, as can infant death. Here is how I chose to handle these situations in one case:

Marie had just turned 23 when she stepped aboard the Frisia *in Hamburg in March of 1884. She was travelling with her entire family, including her mother, stepfather, and six half-siblings. She was also travelling with her baby.*

We don't know anything about the father of her daughter. "Illegitimate" births were very common in Germany at that time, due to a law requiring Community Council approval of every marriage. Many poor young people who could not prove they had the means to support themselves were denied permission to marry or had to wait until a parent passed away and they inherited a farm or business. Perhaps Marie's beloved died and that prompted the desire for a fresh start.

Baby Marie Kruse was born May 15, 1883, while the family was living in Krumbeck, Schleswig-Holstein. She was baptized with the exact same name as her mother, including middle names. Her witnesses were her grandparents, Julius Koch and Maria Koll, as well as Margaretha Schirr. No father was mentioned in the record.

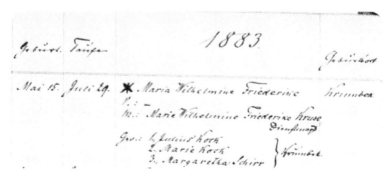

Figure 111: 1883 Marie Wilhelmine Friederike Kruse, Jr. birth

The elder Marie was noted to be a "Diensmagdt," which means "servant girl." Another explanation for the baby's paternity could be that Marie was assaulted by an employer. Marie's future daughter, Alma, warned her own daughter to always wedge a chair against the doorknob at night when she was in service outside the home. It is possible that this lesson was learned in a very real and tragic way by Alma's mother.

Whatever her parentage, baby Marie was only 10 months old when her mother brought her to America for a better life. Heart-breakingly, she would not survive the journey.

The family arrived in New York City on April 8, 1884. Just three days later, baby Marie died at Union Depot after arriving in Milwaukee, Wisconsin.

The coroner interviewed her mother and learned that the baby had gotten sick after their arrival in America. He named "worm disease and exposure while travelling" as the causes of death. She likely contracted worms from drinking contaminated milk during the journey, since pasteurization was not common yet. In addition, the family had very little money and likely travelled in the cheapest passenger train cars they could find. Such conditions would have made it very difficult to care for a sick child. Little Marie was buried in the County Poor Farm Cemetery in Milwaukee. On her death certificate, the space for "Name of Father" read simply "illegitimate." Her sad story was over.

So, when adult Marie arrived in Ozaukee County in April 1884, she was a mother with no child. And baby Johanna Schmidt was a child with no mother. Fate brought them together.

Offering historical context and possible explanations can go a long way toward treating sensitive situations with respect. And respect should always be top of mind when writing a family history.

SOURCES

Citing your sources serves several functions. First, it lends credibility to your research, showing the work you have done and helping the reader feel more confident in what you are saying. Second, it is a finding aid for readers and other researchers who wish to follow in your footsteps.

The book *Evidence Explained* (2007) by Elizabeth Shown Mills is very well-respected in the genealogy community if you are searching for citation guidelines.

BIBLIOGRAPHY

There are many standard formats for bibliographies. I use the one automatically created by FBC. One drawback to my method is that sources from my written biographies are not included automatically in the bibliography, so they must be added manually.

CITATIONS

If you are using Word, you can take advantage of its built-in citation capabilities when writing your biographies. FBC will then incorporate them for you automatically (either as endnotes or footnotes, depending on your selected FBC preferences) when it runs.

TYPES OF CITATIONS

You can choose where your citations will appear. My preferred method is to use endnotes (all citations collected at the very end of the document) rather than footnotes (each citation shown at the bottom of the page where it originated). Footnotes played havoc with my layouts when I had to make edits later and took up a great deal of room on the page.

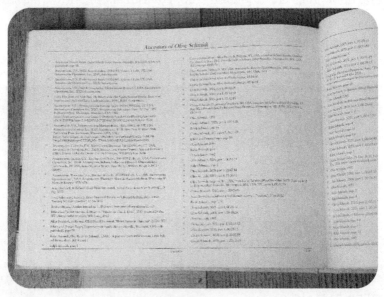

Figure 112: Endnotes in my second book

Citations are also of no interest to a good chunk of my readership – my grandma and her cousins. I did not want to clutter the page with references they would never read, but I did want to have the references in case a fellow researcher really cared and wanted to follow up on something. Therefore, endnotes were the best route for me.

INSERTING CITATIONS (FBC)

In FBC, go to the **Preferences** workspace, then find the *General* tab. In the left column is the *Source Citations* section.

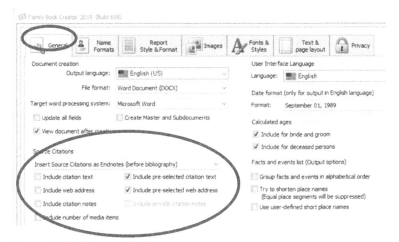

Figure 113: FBC Source Citations

Here you can tell FBC how you would like your information to be cited – i.e., no citations, citations as footnotes, citations as endnotes (two options), or embedded citations.

INSERTING CITATIONS (WORD)

To insert an endnote in your narrative biography or final Word document, open the **References Ribbon** and click *Insert Endnote*. Word will jump

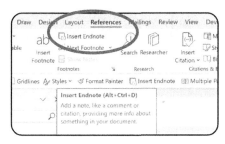

Figure 114: Insert endnote

to the end of your chapter, and you can type or paste in your reference.

Lorem ipsum dolor sit amet, consectetur adipiscing elit, sed do eiusmod tempor incididunt ut labore et dolore magna aliqua. Ut enim ad minim veniam, quis nostrud exercitation ullamco laboris nisi ut aliquip ex ea commodo consequat. Duis aute irure dolor in reprehenderit in voluptate velit esse cillum dolore eu fugiat nulla pariatur. Excepteur sint occaecat cupidatat non proident, sunt in culpa qui officia deserunt mollit anim id est laborum.[i]

[i] Jane Doe, "Very Interesting Article", 1 Jan 2019, *Excellent Newspaper*, accessed 12 Mar 2023

Often, I end up creating the citation in FTM and simply

Figure 115: Example endnote

copying the Reference Note so I can paste directly into Word.

Figure 116: Copying citation from FTM

Don't worry that your endnotes appear at the end of your biography – if you are using FBC, it will renumber and move them to the end of the book with the rest of the endnotes.

> Tip: If you double click the tiny number to the left of an endnote in your document, Word will jump back to the page in question.

CITATION NUMBERING (WORD)

If you are a bit "extra" like me and have hundreds of citations in your book, I recommend using traditional numbers rather than Roman numerals (the default option).

To do this, open the *Footnote and Endnote* menu in the **References Ribbon** by clicking the little arrow in the bottom right corner of the section.

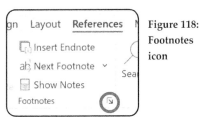

Figure 118: Footnotes icon

Then under "Number format" open the dropdown, change your selection to "1, 2, 3," and click *Apply*.

Figure 117: Footnotes menu

WORKING WITH IMAGES

Images are key to a pleasant reading experience. They provide visual variety and let the reader's eyes rest for a moment. I will share some of my formatting preferences for images in Word, but obviously, there are many ways to edit and show your images.

PREPARING AN IMAGE

I prefer to prepare and crop my images before I bring them into Word, especially census records. This helps keep the total file size down. By the time you have several hundred pages of content, with at least one image per page, you are dealing with a pretty hefty Word document. This slows you down when saving the file, when printing, and when trying to share it with someone else.

> Tip: Another way to limit file size is to compress images (see page 177).

Ideally, your original images will have a resolution of at least 200 pixels per inch (PPI) (300 PPI is better), but lower resolution is not unusual when working with old documents, and most readers will not mind. JPG or JPEG files are easiest to work with in FTM and Word.

CROPPING IMAGES (WINDOWS)

Windows includes editing capabilities in its free default Photos app.

1. To begin, double click the photo in Windows Explorer to open **Photos**.

2. Click the icon with a tiny pencil in front of a photo, near the top left corner of your image.

Figure 119: Photos app in Windows

3. *Crop* should be the default choice. Drag the corners of the image in and out as desired.

Figure 120: Cropping in the Photos app

4. Click the blue *Save as Copy* button to preserve your original image and create a new cropped photo.

Then when you are ready to incorporate this image into your book, make sure to insert your new cropped version.

Always preserve your original files for safekeeping by saving them in a separate folder or hard drive. You never know when you will need that content. As you edit each photo, assign a new name to the file to indicate that it is not the original version.

ADOBE® PHOTOSHOP® FOR EDITING IMAGES

If you have the relevant skills and software, I recommend using Adobe Photoshop software to edit manifests and census records. Photoshop itself requires a monthly subscription and allows for very complex editing, while Adobe Photoshop Elements® is a one-time purchase with simpler, more streamlined options.

Photoshop allows you to cut out your family's information and drag them up to the top of the page, combine family members split across multiple pages, and edit out irrelevant columns of data. You can also improve readability by adjusting White/Black levels, contrast, and clarity.

In this example, Photoshop allowed me to include column headers even though my family was at the bottom of the page, and I was able to crop out columns 18-20 to allow the rest of the data to be displayed at a larger size.

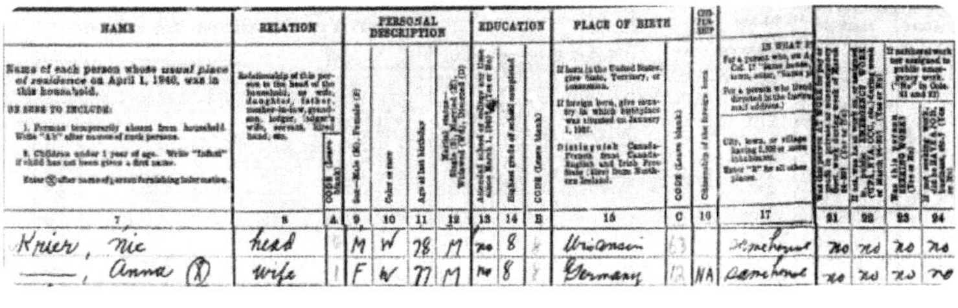

Figure 121: Sample edited census

Census data in particular requires a lot of horizontal space to display, and you should take advantage of any method that allows you to maximize the information presented.

INSERTING AN IMAGE (WORD)

You can copy and paste an image into your document using your keyboard (Ctrl+C and Ctrl+P), or right-clicking to access Copy and Paste Commands. Or you can drag and drop the file from Windows Explorer.

You can also go to the **Insert Ribbon** and choose *Pictures*, then *This Device* to navigate to your edited image file.

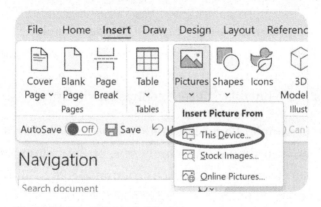

Figure 122: Insert Picture in Word

Tip: Using Copy/Paste will result in the images being inserted at a larger file size. If you are concerned about minimizing total file size, use Insert or drag and drop.

IMAGE LAYOUT OPTIONS (WORD)

The inserted image will likely default to being *In Line with Text*. That means the picture will sit on the line where you inserted it and make that entire line taller to accommodate. I really dislike this layout. I don't like how one line of text has a different height from the rest of the paragraph.

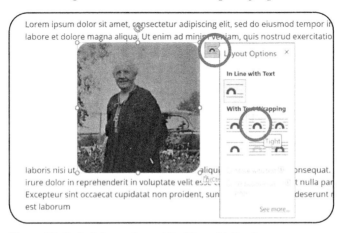

Figure 123: Default Image Layout (In Line with Text)

Text Wrapping offers a more streamlined, professional look. You can access this by clicking on the little rainbow-looking icon outside the upper right corner of your image.

My go-to selection is *Tight* (top middle icon), which means the text will flow along the edges of your image and caption (even when they are grouped).

Figure 124: Tight Text Wrapping

Square (top left icon) is similar to *Tight,* but text flows around the entire group as a whole, based on the widest element.

Another option I use is *Top and Bottom,* which forces text to be above or below the image across the whole page.

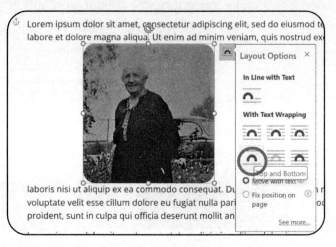

Figure 125: Top and Bottom Text Wrapping

I usually leave my images on "Move with Text" because my layout is fluid, but you can also choose "Fix Position on Page" if you don't want them to move.

These *Wrapping* options really stand out and can be the key to having a professional appearance for your book.

WHERE TO PUT YOUR IMAGES

Choosing where to place images on a page is primarily a matter of personal taste but there are some general guidelines you should consider.

PHASE 3: WRITING

1. Place images on the edges of a page, since flowing text attractively and logically around an image in the middle of a page can be a challenge.

2. Aim for visual variety. If you have an image in the top left corner of page 6, try the bottom right corner of page 7. They do not have to be symmetrical, but each page should be different from (and complementary to) the immediately preceding and following pages.

Figure 126: An example set of pages from my second book

3. Whenever possible, keep images next to the text they are illustrating (see "Image Anchors" on page 162). Otherwise, your reader will have to flip pages back and forth to understand what you are writing about. You can re-size images to ensure they remain on the correct page.

4. Play with moving images up or down (or making them bigger/smaller) to ensure that paragraphs are balanced, avoiding "orphan" words on the last line. Instead of this:

Figure 127: Orphaned text

Try enlarging the image slightly so the text is more balanced on the last line:

Figure 128: More balanced text

Another solution for orphan words is to reword the paragraph or adjust character spacing.

Little details like this can make a difference that a reader doesn't notice directly, but that contributes to a feeling of "rightness" when the reader looks at the entire page.

GRIDLINES (WORD)

Word allows you to place images outside of the margins you have established for the document. To avoid problems, turn on Gridlines in the *Show* section of the **View Ribbon**.

Figure 129: Turn on Gridlines

All images should be within the gridlines. In this example, I can see my image is too far to the left because it is hanging off the grid. So, I need to drag the photo to the right to comply with my margins.

Figure 130: Image off the gridlines

Since Gridlines can be a visual distraction, I usually keep them off until I need them, which is why I add them to my Quick Access Toolbar.

IMAGE ANCHORS (WORD)

This next section is critical to understand if you use images. I would have saved myself *hours* of frustration and gnashing of teeth had I understood image anchors from the start. An anchor is the bit of text (or an object) that an image is "tied" to. If that text is pushed to the next page of the document (perhaps because you added a new paragraph before it), the image will go with that text (even if you picked "Fix Position on Page").

This can be startling and frustrating if you are not prepared for it. You may find yourself dragging images from page to page, and tearing out your hair when they will not stay put.

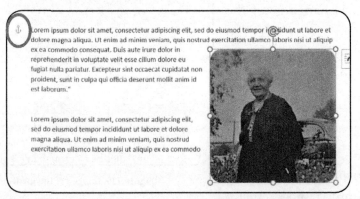

Figure 131: Image is anchored to Paragraph 1

In this example, my image is anchored to the first paragraph. I know this because of the little blue anchor symbol that appeared to the left of the paragraph when I clicked on the image. Note that the anchor is by the text, not the image.

DISPLAYING ANCHORS

If you do not see a blue anchor symbol when you click on an image, you may not have this display option turned on in Word. To enable this, go to **File**, then click *Options* at the bottom of the menu.

Figure 132: File → Options

Click on the *Display* menu and look for *Always show these formatting marks on the screen.* Ensure that *Object anchors* has been checked.

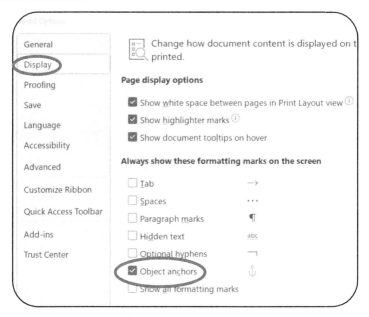

Figure 133: Display Object anchors

If you still don't see an anchor after taking these steps, make sure you have set the Image Layout of that particular image to *Wrapping*.

WHY ANCHORS MATTER

In this example, the image is anchored to Paragraph 1 ("Lorem ipsum…") on this page. I can tell because of the blue anchor symbol.

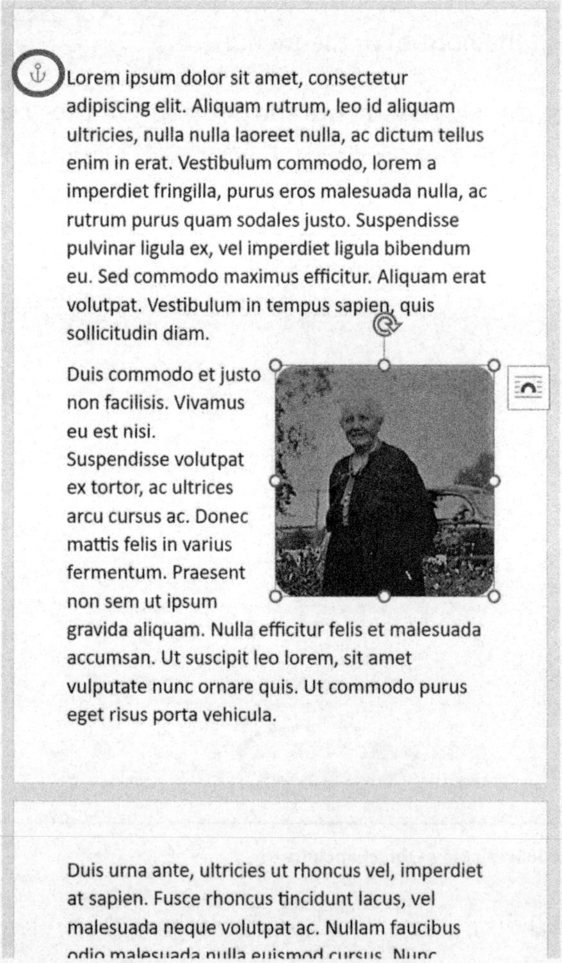

Figure 134: Image anchored to Paragraph 1

If I add new text between the paragraphs, the image will stay on Page 1, because its anchor is still on Page 1. The "Duis commodo" paragraph has been pushed to the next page, but that did not affect my image, since they were not anchored together.

Lorem ipsum dolor sit amet, consectetur adipiscing elit. Aliquam rutrum, leo id aliquam ultricies, nulla nulla laoreet nulla, ac dictum tellus enim in erat. Vestibulum commodo, lorem a imperdiet fringilla, purus eros malesuada nulla, ac rutrum purus quam sodales justo. Suspendisse pulvinar ligula ex, vel imperdiet ligula bibendum eu. Sed commodo maximus efficitur. Aliquam erat volutpat. Vestibulum in tempus sapien, quis sollicitudin diam.

NEW NEW NEW NEW
NEW NEW NEW NEW
NEW NEW NEW NEW
NEW NEW NEW NEW
NEW NEW NEW NEW
NEW NEW NEW NEW
NEW NEW NEW NEW
NEW NEW NEW NEW
NEW NEW NEW NEW
NEW NEW NEW NEW NEW NEW NEW NEW NEW
NEW NEW NEW NEW NEW

Lorem ipsum dolor sit amet, consectetur adipiscing elit. Aliquam rutrum, leo id aliquam ultricies, nulla nulla laoreet nulla, ac dictum tellus enim in erat. Vestibulum commodo, lorem a imperdiet fringilla, purus eros malesuada nulla, ac rutrum purus quam sodales justo. Suspendisse pulvinar ligula ex, vel imperdiet ligula bibendum eu. Sed commodo maximus efficitur. Aliquam erat volutpat. Vestibulum in tempus sapien, quis sollicitudin diam.

Duis commodo et justo non facilis. Vivamus eu est nisi. Suspendisse volutpat ex tortor, ac ultrices arcu cursus ac. Donec mattis felis in varius fermentum. Praesent non sem ut ipsum gravida aliquam. Nulla efficitur felis et malesuada accumsan. Ut suscipit leo lorem, sit amet vulputate nunc ornare quis. Ut commodo purus eget risus porta vehicula.

...odo et justo non facilis. Vivamus eu

Figure 135: Image stays put

However, let's start over and change the anchor point to the second paragraph (by clicking, dragging, and dropping the blue anchor next to it).

If I take the same action, inserting some new text

Figure 136: Start over with new anchor

165

in between the two paragraphs, watch what happens to the image this time.

Ack! When my anchor "Duis" paragraph overflowed onto the next page, it took the image along with it.

This is actually a good thing, and what you would want to happen for an image that was intentionally anchored. If that image is a 1900 census record, I want it to *stay* with my discussion of the 1900 census.

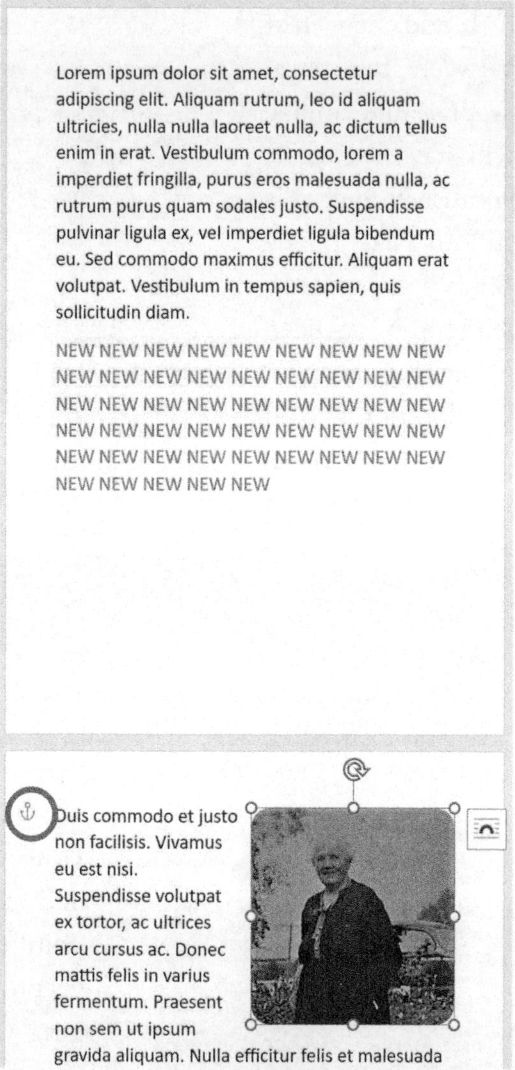

Lorem ipsum dolor sit amet, consectetur adipiscing elit. Aliquam rutrum, leo id aliquam ultricies, nulla nulla laoreet nulla, ac dictum tellus enim in erat. Vestibulum commodo, lorem a imperdiet fringilla, purus eros malesuada nulla, ac rutrum purus quam sodales justo. Suspendisse pulvinar ligula ex, vel imperdiet ligula bibendum eu. Sed commodo maximus efficitur. Aliquam erat volutpat. Vestibulum in tempus sapien, quis sollicitudin diam.

NEW NEW NEW NEW NEW NEW NEW NEW NEW NEW NEW NEW NEW NEW NEW NEW NEW NEW NEW NEW NEW NEW NEW NEW NEW NEW NEW NEW NEW NEW NEW NEW NEW NEW NEW NEW NEW NEW NEW NEW NEW NEW NEW NEW NEW NEW NEW NEW NEW NEW NEW NEW NEW NEW NEW

Duis commodo et justo non facilisis. Vivamus eu est nisi. Suspendisse volutpat ex tortor, ac ultrices arcu cursus ac. Donec mattis felis in varius fermentum. Praesent non sem ut ipsum gravida aliquam. Nulla efficitur felis et malesuada

Figure 137: Image jumps to next page

But if you don't understand anchors, and Word has randomly guessed which paragraph to anchor your image to, you will be confused and frustrated when your image seems to randomly hop to the next page. Save yourself the heartbreak and learn to understand anchors!

Sometimes your image will pop up in a completely different place on the new page, so you will need to drag it into the proper position. This is especially troublesome if the image is too large to fit at the bottom of the page. In that case, I will sometimes insert a manual page break before the anchor text to force the issue. Or, I will re-attach the image to anchor onto the following paragraph so it stays on the next page where it fits.

CROPPING IMAGES (WORD)

Word has built-in cropping features that are handy in a pinch. I prefer to crop outside the program, but sometimes I just want to tweak an image slightly so the text will flow more smoothly around it. Another reason to crop within Word would be if you are not sure exactly how much of the image you want to remove. In Word, you can change your mind and "uncrop" if needed, since the data is not deleted permanently.

Figure 138: Cropping in Word

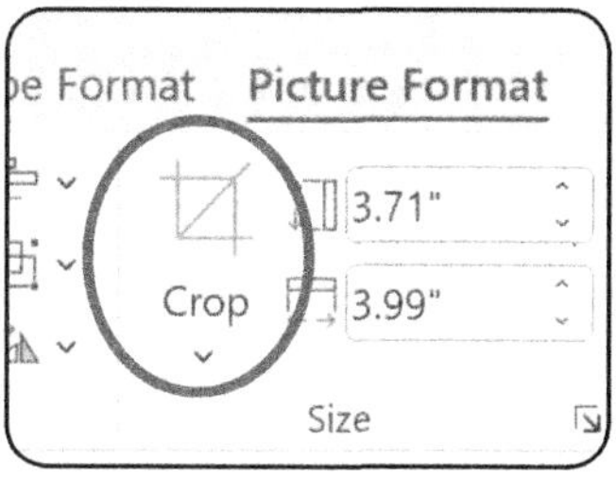

To crop, click on the image, then open the **Picture Format Ribbon** (if you don't see that as an option, you probably forgot to click on the image first).

Then click *Crop*, and black marks will appear around your image. Click and drag them in and out to crop your image.

To finish, simply click anywhere in your document that is outside of the image you were cropping.

Figure 139: Cropping in Word

The result may do strange things to your layout (note the words pushed to the right side of the image below), so you may need to drag the image back to the edge where you would like it. If it is not dragging when you click and drag, you probably forgot to set its Image Layout to *Wrapping*.

Figure 140: Cropped Image in Word

FORMATTING IMAGES (WORD)

You can format your pictures in multiple ways using Word. Unfortunately for me, my preferred style isn't one of the default ones. I like a rounded corner, with no shadows or reflections. The only way I have found of doing that is this:

1. Click the image to open the **Picture Format Ribbon**.

2. Click on the style *Reflected Rounded Rectangle*.

Figure 141: Choosing a default Picture Format style

3. Click on the *Picture Effects* dropdown, then select *Reflection* and finally *No Reflection*.

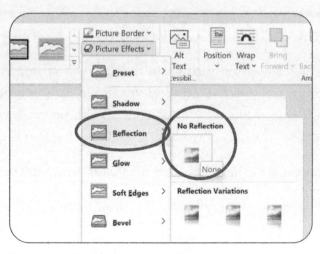

Figure 142: Adjusting picture reflection

If this seems absurdly complicated, that's because it is. I don't know of any other method, but I would sincerely love to be proven wrong. You can save yourself a few clicks if you add these menus to your Quick Access Toolbar, at least.

FORMAT PAINTER (WORD)

After I have done this for one photo, I use Format Painter to copy and paste the formatting to the next image. To do this, click on the formatted image, click on the *Format Painter* button on the **Home Ribbon**, and then click on the new image you would like to format.

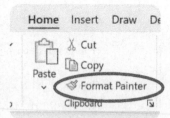

Figure 143: Format Painter

> Tip: If you double-click on the *Format Painter* instead of single-clicking, it will keep working on every image you click on thereafter until you press the Escape key.

If you have advanced knowledge of Word and Visual Basic programming, you can use a macro to copy image formatting to every image in a document.

CAPTIONING IMAGES (WORD)

It is good practice to have a caption for every image in your book. It directs the reader on interpreting what they see, makes it easier to skim, and sets you up for an Index of Figures at the end if you want it.

Right-click on the image and select *Insert Caption*. You can type directly into this caption box in the pop-up window. I like to add a colon after the Figure number, because many of my

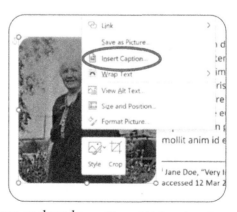

Figure 144: Insert caption

captions begin with a year or decade, and I found the adjacent numbers to be confusing.

Word lets you choose labels other than the word "Figure," but I like that default choice.

Figure 145: Typing a caption

Make sure you pick a general format for your captions in the book (like the way I start all mine with a year). Are you capitalizing the word "Census"? Adding periods in "U.S."? Whatever you choose, be consistent.

Temporarily adding an Index of Figures to your document is an easy way to quickly compare all of your citations and ensure

Figure 146: Image with caption

consistency. To do this, go to the **References Ribbon**, in the *Captions* section, and click *Insert Table of Figures*.

ADJUSTING CAPTIONS (WORD)

Once the caption has been created, you can adjust it like any other text box. Click on the caption and drag the little circles around to shorten or lengthen the caption or increase its height to create more space between it and the document text. You can also change its alignment from Left to Right.

I prefer my captions to be below my image, rather than overlaying it, but you can adjust that as well. If you need to, you can change the font to white to make it stand out against a dark photograph. Remember to create a Style for your preferred caption formatting.

If you are trying to click on the caption but the cursor is just treating it like regular text instead of a box you can adjust, you probably forgot to set the Image Layout to *Wrapping*. Delete that caption, fix the Image Layout, and try again.

Figure 1: This caption is for an image not set for Text Wrapping

Figure 147: Caption for a non-Wrapped image

GROUPING IMAGES AND CAPTIONS (WORD)

In a straightforward book, I usually do not bother to group my images and captions. But if I have to go back and make significant edits (like adding or subtracting content) that are shifting my page layouts, sometimes I will group them just to ensure that they don't get separated in the process.

To do this, click on the caption, then hold down the Control key and click on the image. You will see them each bordered by rectangles marked by circles on the corners and edges.

If this is not working for you, make sure you have turned on *Wrapping* for the image and that it's not *In Line with Text*.

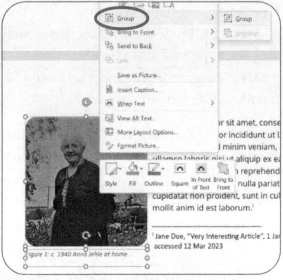

Figure 148: Grouping captions

Then right-click on the combo and select *Group*, then *Group* again.

From now on, they will stick together wherever they are moved. You can see the two rectangles with open circles have changed into one large rectangle around both of them.

Figure 149: Grouped captions

This may have an effect on image wrapping. If you chose *Square* wrapping, Word will flow text around the group as a whole, even if you have shortened the caption box to be narrower than the image. Switch to *Tight* wrapping if you want to make use of that extra space.

174

Tip: If you use *Format Painter* to try and copy the rounded corners formatting and paste to an image that has already been grouped with a caption, strange things can happen, like filling the caption box with a background color. This is another reason I don't group unless needed.

FIXING FIGURE NUMBERS

The easiest way to fix incorrect figure numbers in general is to go to Print Preview, as Word will renumber everything before it prints. However, this solution will not always work for images that use *Wrapping*.

In this situation, the problem is most often where the captions have been anchored. If an image caption is anchored to text higher on the page, it will be numbered before an image caption that is anchored to text lower on the page – *no matter where the images themselves have been placed*.

In the following example, I inserted the photo of the woman before the photo of the man, so the figure numbers reflect that order. She and her caption were anchored to the first paragraph, and he to the second.

But then I decided to move his picture higher on the page, and now they are mixed up. He should now be Figure 1, but Word does not know that. All Word knows is that the woman's caption is anchored earlier, so she gets to be #1.

Lorem ipsum dolor sit amet, consectetur adipiscing elit, sed do eiusmod tempor incididunt ut labore et dolore magna aliqua. Ut enim ad minim veniam, quis nostrud exercitation ullamco laboris nisi ut aliquip ex ea commodo consequat. Duis aute irure dolor in reprehenderit in voluptate velit esse cillum dolore eu fugiat nulla pariatur. Excepteur sint occaecat cupidatat non proident, sunt in culpa qui officia deserunt mollit anim id est laborum

Lorem ipsum dolor sit amet, consectetur adipiscing elit, sed do eiusmod tempor incididunt ut labore et dolore magna aliqua. Ut enim ad minim veniam, quis nostrud exercitation ullamco laboris nisi ut aliquip ex ea commodo consequat. Duis aute irure dolor in reprehenderit in voluptate velit esse cillum dolore eu fugiat nulla pariatur. Excepteur sint occaecat cupidatat non proident, sunt in culpa qui officia deserunt mollit anim id est laborum

Lorem ipsum dolor sit amet, consectetur adipiscing elit, sed do eiusmod tempor incididunt ut labore et dolore magna aliqua. Ut enim ad minim veniam, quis nostrud exercitation ullamco laboris nisi ut aliquip ex ea commodo consequat. Duis aute irure dolor in reprehenderit in voluptate velit esse cillum dolore eu fugiat nulla pariatur. Excepteur sint occaecat cupidatat non proident, sunt in culpa qui officia deserunt mollit anim id est laborum

Lorem ipsum dolor sit amet, consectetur adipiscing elit, sed do eiusmod tempor incididunt ut labore et dolore magna aliqua. Ut enim ad minim veniam, quis nostrud exercitation ullamco laboris nisi ut aliquip ex ea commodo consequat. Duis aute irure dolor in reprehenderit in voluptate

Figure 2:

Figure 1:

Figure 150: Incorrect figure numbers

Print Preview will fix nothing until I fix my anchors. If I drag the woman's caption anchor to the second paragraph, and the man's anchor to the first, and *then* try Print Preview, all will be well.

> Tip: Images and captions each have their own anchors. Make sure to adjust the anchor for the caption itself, or both grouped together.

COMPRESSING IMAGES (WORD)

If your Word document is growing very large and unwieldy, you can compress its images to cut down the file size.

1. First, click on an image.

2. Under the **Picture Format Ribbon** in the *Adjust* section, click on *Compress Pictures*.

Figure 151: Picture Format Ribbon

3. To compress all images in the document, uncheck *Apply only to this picture*. To make the file even smaller, check *Delete cropped areas of pictures* (if you are sure you will not need to adjust those crops later).

Figure 152: Compress Pictures

4. Select your desired resolution (220 PPI is a good choice for print) and click *OK*.

INDEXES (WORD/FBC)

Many word processing programs, including Word, have an indexing function. It requires advanced knowledge of text markup, but there is a shortcut if you use FBC.

FBC has a very cool feature in which it automatically creates an Index of Places and an Index of Individuals (see page 102). You have the option of including your biographies in these indexes if you are willing to put in the work. In my first book, I simply made a note above the index explaining that the biographies were not included. With my second book, I put in the additional time and effort.

In order for a name or a place in the narrative biography to be included in the Index of Names or Index of Places, you will need to have a (practice) Word document produced by FBC in order to copy the exact mark-up code. Make sure you are adding these codes to the individual couple's Word document, not your final book. Otherwise your additions will be lost when you run FBC again at the end of your writing process.

First, start by clicking *Show All* to display field codes in your practice document. Find a Family Chart or Summary page and look for the person or place you want to index. Copy the code appearing after the name in the curly brackets { }. Make sure you include the brackets.

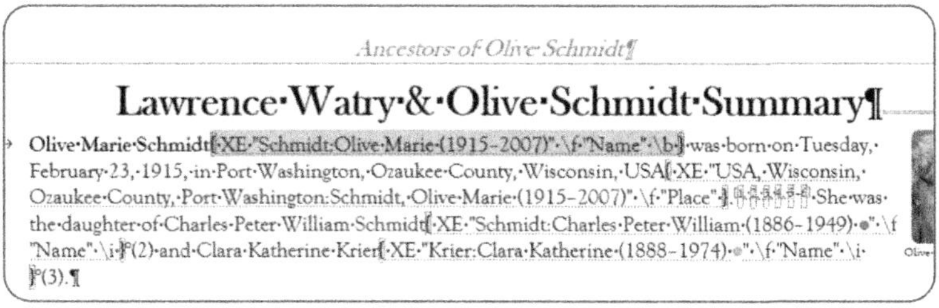

PHASE 3: WRITING

Figure 153: Copying person markup code

Then find your biography chapter and paste this code after the place or person's name.

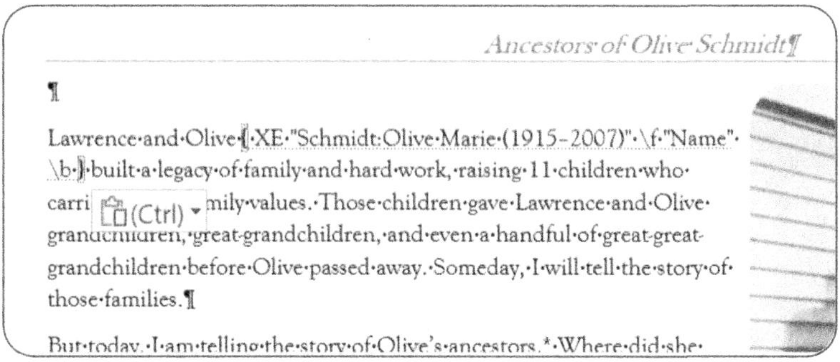

Figure 154: Adding person markup code

If you want to use a name that doesn't already appear in the FBC-created file, you can copy and paste the same code (within the curly brackets), but manually type over the name and range of birth/death years within the quotation marks, using the *exact format* shown.

Alternatively, you can place your cursor at the appropriate spot, hit Ctrl + F9 to create a field code, then type within the curly brackets that appear (do not simply type the curly brackets yourself, as the necessary code will not be embedded that way).

If you have an advanced understanding of Word and know how to construct an index from scratch, you could do that instead, but it may not integrate smoothly with the index created by FBC, so copying and pasting the code as described here will likely be simpler.

When you turn off *Show All*, you will not be able to see the markup text that you just added, but this page will now be included for that person's name in the Index of Individuals (or for that place in the Index of Places). Be sure not to accidentally paste an extra space on either side of the brackets, which will look odd in the final document.

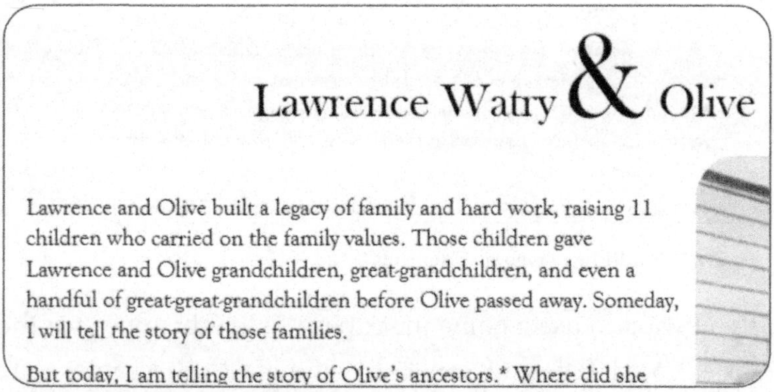

Lawrence Watry & Olive

Lawrence and Olive built a legacy of family and hard work, raising 11 children who carried on the family values. Those children gave Lawrence and Olive grandchildren, great-grandchildren, and even a handful of great-great-grandchildren before Olive passed away. Someday, I will tell the story of those families.

But today, I am telling the story of Olive's ancestors.* Where did she

Figure 155: Markup disappears when you turn off *Show All*

This can be a lot of work in some cases, so you can make the decision to only index the main couple in a chapter, or only index them and their parents. I simply added a note in the Index section that siblings and others were not indexed in the biographies.

LAYOUT TIPS (WORD)

VIEW (WORD)

I am a photographer, so I have an enormous computer screen that I use for editing. This means I have a lot of visual space to work with, so I make sure to set my document zoom to a percent that matches up to the real-life size of my book pages (for me, that is 95%).

In Word, you can drag the *Zoom* bar back and forth across the lower right corner of the screen to adjust your view.

Figure 156: Page Zoom in Word

> Tip: Try actually holding a real sheet of paper up to your screen and adjusting the zoom until the digital image matches the real page.

It is okay to zoom in sometimes to work with something in detail, but make sure to go back to "real life" frequently so you can see how something will really appear to the reader. Mostly, this strategy is important to make sure you keep your font and images large enough to be legible.

MULTIPLE PAGES (WORD)

You can also set your view to be across *Multiple Pages*. This is helpful for getting a bird's-eye view of your document and how it flows. Pages are read across and then down.

Figure 157: Multiple Page View in Word

If you decrease your Zoom, you can see a dozen or more pages at once.

To do this in Word, look on the **View Ribbon** for *Multiple Pages*. You can click *One Page* to go back to the previous view.

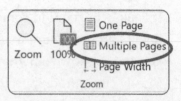

Figure 158: Zoom menu in Word

LEFT & RIGHT PAGES

Some word processors (including Word) have an absolutely maddening lack of ability to see a document as it would be laid out in a book. A printed book begins on the right-hand side, not the left. So, in the previous example, that title page "Ancestors of Olive Marie Schmidt" is actually printed on the right side of the real book, but it is page 1 in Word, which puts it on the left side in *Multiple Pages* View.

This feature makes it very difficult to visualize your page flow if you work in *Multiple Pages* View. Page-side matters to me, because I like every new generation to begin on the right side, and every family section to start on the left side.

Figure 159: First page of my book

You can see proper page sides in Print Preview, but I prefer being able to edit and see my changes appear live.

Figure 160: Starting family sections on the left

> Tip: A workaround to this issue is to insert a blank page at the very beginning of your final compiled document, to falsely move everything to the proper position.
>
> *IMPORTANT: You must delete that temporary blank page before printing.*
>
> This is critical. Otherwise, your final product will be completely wrong anyway. Also, be sure to update your Table of Contents and any indexes after you delete it, or your page numbers will all be off by one (see page 191 for instructions on how to do this).

This, by the way, is a great example of why it is wise to leave yourself extra time at the end of the book creation process to catch high-level mistakes such as these.

TIMESAVERS (WORD)

Many formatting tasks can feel tedious when you have to repeat them over and over, but there are shortcuts you can build in to save time and frustration.

STYLES (WORD)

Word has a built-in feature that allows you to save certain formatting as a "style," making it easier to apply it elsewhere in your document. Styles are also essential for having Word configure your Table of Contents.

I found this feature incredibly helpful for captions. I wanted my captions to be either left- or right-aligned, depending on their placement in the document. I was able to save each option style (as well as a white font option, for captions overlying photographs) and simply select them as needed.

To create a caption style, do the following:

1. Insert a caption as usual.

2. Click on your caption, and make sure you are in the **Home Ribbon**.

3. Find the *Styles* section and click the down-facing caret with the line over it (not the angled arrow) near the bottom right corner.

Figure 161: Style section in the Home Ribbon

4. Then click *Create a Style*.

Figure 162: Click "Create a Style"

5. In the pop-up, click *Modify*.

Figure 163: Modify the Style

6. Make the formatting changes you'd like, such as shifting to Right Alignment, name your new style, and click *OK*.

Figure 164: Formatting the new Style

7. This style will now appear in the *Styles* section on your **Home Ribbon**.

Figure 165: New Style in the Home Ribbon

8. Repeat these steps for a left or center alignment, adding variations in different font colors if you like.

Next time you want to format a caption, just click on the style you want from the **Home Ribbon**.

MAKING STYLE CHANGES

The best thing about using this method (as opposed to manually changing format each time) is that you can go back and change everything all at once later. Have you suddenly decided that all captions should be in italics? Simply modify that Style, and boom, the entire document is updated.

The simplest way to do this is to select some text using that Style, and make the changes you want. Then go to the Styles menu and right-click on the Style name and choose *Update [YourStyleName] to Match Selection*.

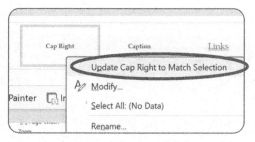

Figure 166: Updating Styles

Tip: If you are using Styles and decide to make formatting changes to a specific caption, make sure to do so by selecting a new Style (rather than manually changing that caption). If you manually change it, sometimes this can affect other captions that inherit features from that Style.

NAVIGATION PANE (WORD)

Using Styles also enables you to use the Navigation Pane, which helps you quickly move around your document even when it is very long and complex. In the **View Ribbon**, look for the *Show* section and check *Navigation Pane*.

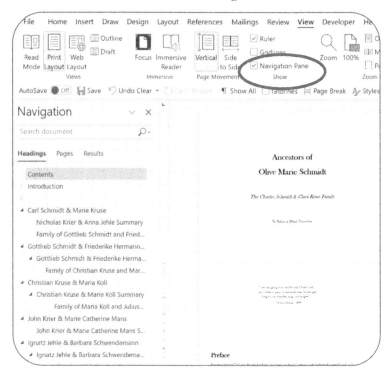

Figure 167: Navigation Pane

The pane will appear on the left side of the screen. Clicking on a heading in the pane allows you to jump to different sections of your book without having to scroll all the way back up to the Table of Contents to find them.

QUICK ACCESS TOOLBAR (WORD)

Are there tools that you frequently use in Word, but you get
tired of clicking through all the
ribbons and menus to access
them? You can add shortcuts
directly to your main display. To
do this, right-click on an icon in

Figure 168: Add to Quick Access Toolbar

any Ribbon and select *Add to Quick Access Toolbar*.

Here are some shortcuts that I use:

Figure 169: Example Quick Access Toolbar

I also have shortcuts for certain macros that I have written.
A macro is a small piece of computer code that lets you
automate certain repetitive actions, such as formatting.

Sometimes, certain Quick Access options will be grayed out
because they are only applicable in certain situations (e.g.,
when you have clicked on an image).

This tip is surprisingly helpful. Once you start using this
toolbar, you will wonder how you ever got by without it.

UPDATE FIELDS

If you are using a Table of Contents or indexes, you will need to periodically update them as your book changes. To update a single table, right click on the table and select *Update Field*.

Figure 170: Update field

If you have added, deleted, or changed any headings in your document, Word will ask whether you want to update just the page numbers for existing items, or update the entire table to reflect the greater changes. In most cases, you should update the entire table.

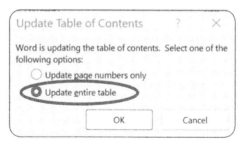

Figure 171: Update ToC

To update all fields in the document at once, press Ctrl+A and then F9.

If you are concerned that you may forget to update your fields before printing, you can set Word to do this automatically for you. Go to **File →** **Options → Display**. Then under *Printing options*, check *Update fields before printing*.

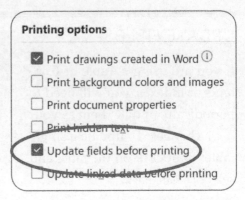

Figure 172: Update fields before printing

DISPLAY HIDDEN SYMBOLS (WORD)

Are your paragraphs behaving strangely, with surprising page breaks or indents? There is a way to see the "rules" that are governing that layout.

To see the hidden formatting symbols, click on *Show All* (or *Show/Hide* in Office 2019). You will find this in the **Home Ribbon**, under the

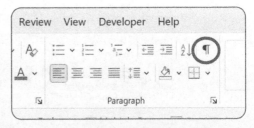

Figure 173: Turning on Show All

Paragraph section. It looks like a little paragraph mark, and it functions as an on/off toggle button. This will display markup tags next to your text. These can include tabs, paragraph breaks, spaces, and more.

For example, you might notice that some paragraphs are not indented consistently. In this example, the second paragraph is not indented as far as the others.

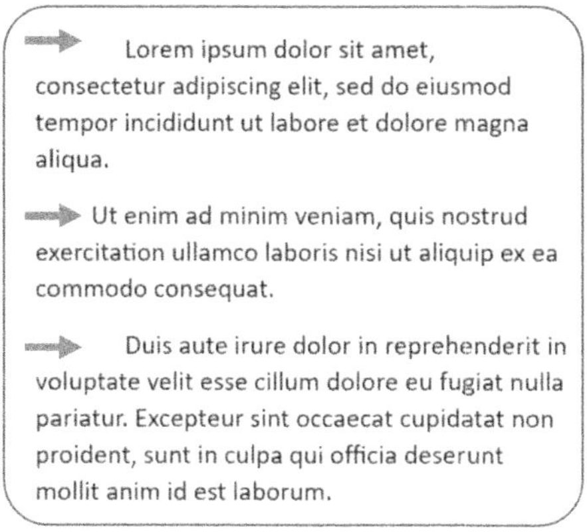
Lorem ipsum dolor sit amet, consectetur adipiscing elit, sed do eiusmod tempor incididunt ut labore et dolore magna aliqua.

Ut enim ad minim veniam, quis nostrud exercitation ullamco laboris nisi ut aliquip ex ea commodo consequat.

Duis aute irure dolor in reprehenderit in voluptate velit esse cillum dolore eu fugiat nulla pariatur. Excepteur sint occaecat cupidatat non proident, sunt in culpa qui officia deserunt mollit anim id est laborum.

Figure 174: Inconsistent

However, when we turn on "Show All" and examine the formatting marks, we can see that instead of a proper Tab, a series of spaces was manually inserted before "Ut," leading to the inconsistency. With this information, we can delete the spaces and replace them with an appropriate Tab.

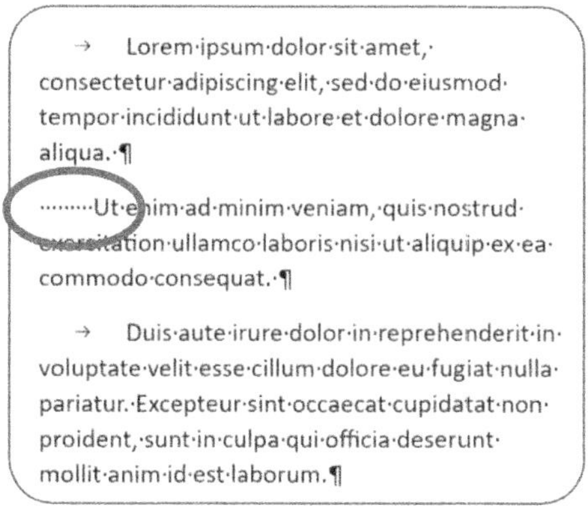
→ Lorem·ipsum·dolor·sit·amet,· consectetur·adipiscing·elit,·sed·do·eiusmod· tempor·incididunt·ut·labore·et·dolore·magna· aliqua.·¶

········Ut·enim·ad·minim·veniam,·quis·nostrud· exercitation·ullamco·laboris·nisi·ut·aliquip·ex·ea· commodo·consequat.·¶

→ Duis·aute·irure·dolor·in·reprehenderit·in· voluptate·velit·esse·cillum·dolore·eu·fugiat·nulla· pariatur.·Excepteur·sint·occaecat·cupidatat·non· proident,·sunt·in·culpa·qui·officia·deserunt· mollit·anim·id·est·laborum.¶

Figure 175: "Show All" reveals

Don't be concerned that turning on *Show All* has destroyed all of your careful layout work. Everything you see is temporary, and when you hide the markup tags again, it will all go back to where it was.

DISPLAY FIELD CODES

Another type of hidden symbol that appears with *Show All* is that of field codes. These markups govern how Word creates internal references in your document, such as for a Table of Contents or an index. You will see them between curly brackets { }, as below.

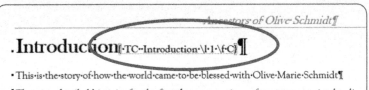

Figure 176: Show All markup

In this example, the field code explains that this line is in the Table of Contents ("TC"), with the text "Introduction," on Level 1 ("l-1"), in the specific table labelled as "C" (in case there are multiple tables in the document).

One way to toggle field codes alone (without the rest of the formatting symbols) on a PC is to hit Alt+F9 (then hit Alt+F9 again to toggle off).

Field codes are not visible in your final document, but they are the foundation of automated features like indexes (see page 178.

ADD COLUMNS (WORD)

There may be some sections of your book that call for content to be split into multiple vertical columns, rather than continuing unbroken across the entire page. This can be especially appropriate if you use landscape orientation. I prefer to use three columns in my indexes and two columns for my endnotes.

To do this in Word, select the paragraphs in question. Then go to the **Layout Ribbon** and find the *Page Setup* section. Click on "Columns" to choose the number of columns. Word will adjust your layout accordingly.

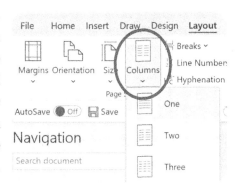

Figure 177: Columns in Word

KEEP TEXT TOGETHER (WORD)

When writing your book, there may be certain content that you wish to keep together rather than being split onto different pages. This could mean specific lines of text within a single paragraph, or it could mean multiple paragraphs that you'd like to keep together on the same page.

To do this, first select the text in question. Go to the **Home Ribbon** and find the *Paragraph* section. Click on the little arrow in the bottom right corner (to save time in the future, add this to your Quick Access Toolbar).

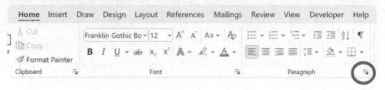

Figure 178: Paragraph settings in Word

Within the *Line and Page Breaks* tab, there are several options. The first one, "Widow/Orphan control", makes sure that the first or last line of text in a paragraph is never left all alone at the top or bottom of a page or column. I keep this option selected by default for everything I write.

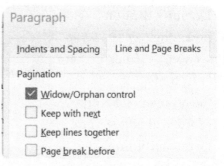

Figure 179: Line and Page Breaks

The next two options are how we control keeping important content together. They are often confused or conflated, but here is the difference:

"Keep with next" ensures that multiple *paragraphs* are kept together on the same page.

"Keep lines together" ensures that multiple *lines* of text within a *single* paragraph are kept together (so the paragraph will not split across two pages).

Why don't they just label them "Keep Paragraphs Together" and "Keep Lines Together"? It is a mystery.

These features can be particularly helpful when creating short lists of items that should be kept together, as well as ensuring that a heading is not separated from its following paragraph.

"Keep with next" can actually be added to the heading's Style so you do not have to select it manually. To do this from the "Create new style from formatting" or "Modify Style" pop-ups (see page 188), click the *Format* button at the bottom left of the pop-up and select *Paragraph*. Then go to the *Line and Page Breaks* tab and check the appropriate boxes.

Figure 180: Format button in Style pop-up

Tip: This method is preferred over inserting manual Page Breaks, because it is more resilient to later editing. A "hard" Page Break remains in effect even if content is later added or removed such that it produces a blank page in the middle of a chapter. Using "Keep with next" or "Keep lines together" instead means that action is only taken to group content with a page break if it is truly needed.

CREATE THE EXTRAS

If you are using FBC and have extra content, compile it all into a "Conclusion" Word document and attach it in FTM to the last person in your book, just as you attached the biographies. In order to ensure the Conclusion is inserted after all of the last couple's data, do *not* select the media categories for placement before or after the family chart.

MAPS (GOOGLE MAPS)

I use Google "My Maps" to create a custom map with markers on it for each place my ancestors came from:

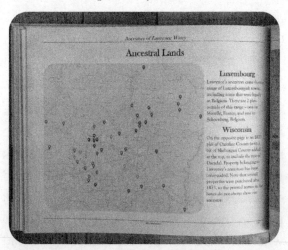

Figure 181: Ancestral Homeland page in my book

I also plan to use this map someday when I finally get to visit Europe and see my ancestral homelands.

198

PHASE 3: WRITING

1. Create a layer for this ancestor. Layer visibility can be turned on and off.

    a. I make each great-grandparent its own layer, so I can have separate maps for separate books but still have everything in one place.

    b. I included six generations for this exercise.

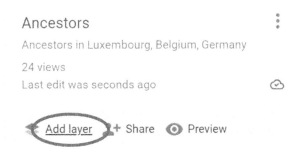

Figure 182: Add layer in Google My Maps

2. Search for a town or location that your ancestor is from and select a result.

Figure 183: Search for a town

3. Click on the green marker that appears, then click *Add to Map* in the bottom left corner of the popup.

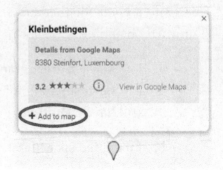

Figure 184: Add to map

4. Click on the pencil icon to edit the marker settings.

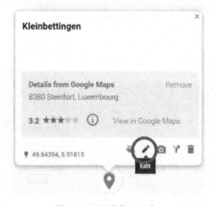

Figure 185: Edit marker settings

5. You can rename the marker if you choose. I like to add more information about the location to the title. I also add notes about which family lines have been found in that town.

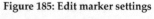

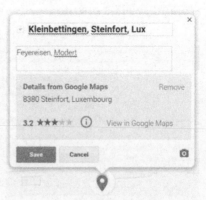

Figure 186: Rename marker

6. To color-code the map, click the little paint bucket icon. I try to echo the FTM color-code scheme.

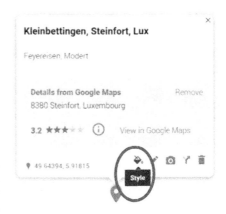

Figure 187: Edit marker style

7. Finally, click and drag to re-order entries in your layer. I prefer to group colors so I can see the family lines at a glance.

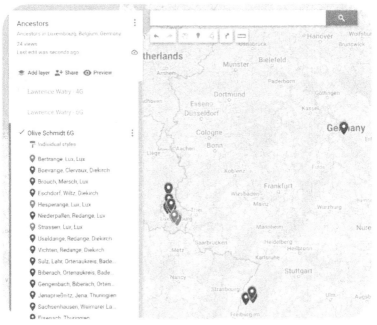

Figure 188: Example Google My Maps for ancestors

This is a very manual process, but I love the results. And I love that they will be helpful when I travel there someday.

> Tip: You can share a direct link to this map with other people (for example, readers).

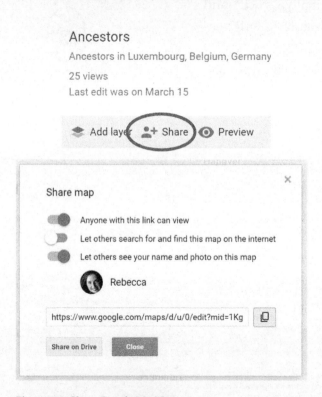

Figure 189: Share Google My Maps

WORD CLOUDS

I didn't use a word cloud in my last book, but if you want to, I recommend using the site www.wordclouds.com. One nice feature they have is the ability to choose a tree as the shape of your word cloud.

Figure 190: Word cloud shapes

Figure 191: WordClouds.com

I created a list of surnames from my tree in Excel, then I copied and repeatedly pasted the ones that I wanted to be bigger than the rest. I used that as my Word List, then played with colors and fonts until I liked the results.

Figure 192: My family tree word cloud

FAN CHARTS (CHARTING COMPANION)

I used another FTM plug-in to create the 7-generation fan chart for my book. The plug-in is called "Charting Companion 8" (CC8).

From within the plug-in, click on the *Charts and Reports* menu, and select *Ancestor Fan Chart*.

There are many ways to customize your chart, but I will share my settings here.

Figure 193: Ancestor Fan Chart in CC8

I used Goudy Old Style 9pt regular font, to match the font style in the charts in my book.

I prefer a simple, clean look, so I do not use any borders or background images.

Figure 194: Content tab in CC8

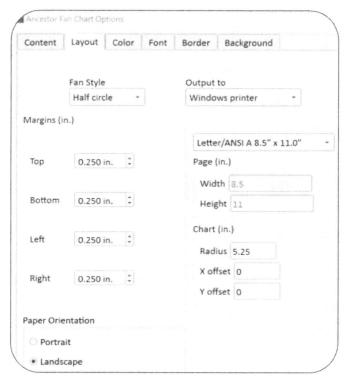

Figure 195: Layout tab in CC8

For my first book, I manually edited the colors for each generation. This took a lot of effort, so in my next book, I left the colors as plain black & white, and shifted the colors later when editing my cover using Photoshop.

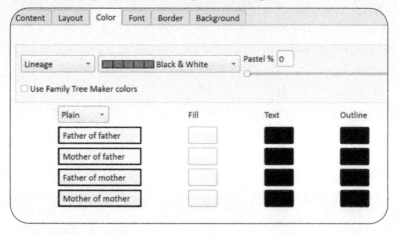

Figure 196: Color tab in CC8

When you are happy with your chart, you can insert it into your Conclusions Word doc with the other extras.

Figure 197:
My fan chart

PHASE 4:
PRINTING

4

If you are using FBC, run it one last time and commit to making any remaining edits to your final complete document rather than the individual biographies. Then prepare for printing!

FINAL REVIEW

Before exporting your book for print, you should take time to do one final review. Consider checking the following overall elements:

1. Make sure every figure has a caption and that figure numbers are in correct order (page 175).
2. Review left/right page layouts and make sure there are no accidental blank pages. Delete the blank first page if you added one (page 183).
3. Make sure all text and images are within the gridlines (page 161).
4. Do a final spelling and grammar check.
5. Ensure that *Show All* is toggled off and then update Indexes and your Table of Contents (page 191).
6. Spot-check the Index page numbers and Table of Contents page numbers to make sure they are correct with your pagination.
7. Review the draft again several days later. It is amazing how often you catch issues when you look again with a pair of fresh eyes.

EXPORTING FOR PRINT

PDF SETTINGS (WORD)

Most print companies ask you to upload a PDF of your document, rather than a .docx. *If you do not have a colored/image background on your pages*, you can export your document directly from Word.

An easy way to do this is through **File** → *Save As*. Choose *PDF* as your "Save as type," but before you click the *Save* button, click on the *Options* button.

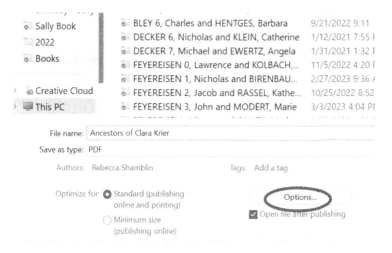

Figure 198: Save As PDF

Make sure you check the box for "PDF/A compliant." If your printer rejects your file (especially if they tell you that the fonts need to be embedded), try going back to this step and making sure you check that box.

After you do it once, it should stay checked, so you will not have to select it every time.

Be sure to leave extra time for this step and check each page of your final PDF for any irregularities introduced by the process.

Figure 199: Save As PDF Options

PDF SETTINGS (PDF X-CHANGE)

The following information took me *weeks* to figure out. I spent untold hours talking with various customer service representatives trying to untangle the problem of having a colored or full image background on my pages in Word.

I specifically wanted a background image so my books

Figure 200: Parchment background by Etsy seller OpticIllusions

looked as though they were printed on old paper. I purchased a parchment-style digital backdrop on Etsy.com and reduced its opacity to 25% to use it as a background for all my pages.

Tip: Printing in color is considerably more expensive than printing in black & white. Keep this in mind when choosing a colored or image background.

If you are using a colored page background or an image for your page backgrounds, you cannot export to PDF in the usual way. Word has a known bug related to this feature, and I have yet to find a workaround. If you try it, you will get a PDF with white lines down the right side and along the bottom of every page.

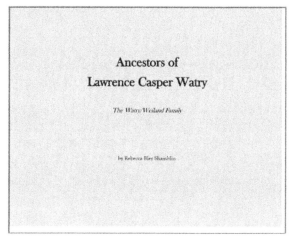

Figure 201: Bug when exporting colored backgrounds in Word

The only solution I have found to this day is to purchase software called "PDF X-Change Editor" (since this is a PC-only application, I unfortunately do not have a solution for Mac users). You will need to use the premium version, not the free version.

Wait to add the background until after exporting to PDF.

Using PDF X-Change:

1. Remove the background in Word (if it has already been added), whether it is a color or an image. Save the document *and close it*. The file cannot be open in Word during this process.

2. Next, open PDF X-Change. Drag the Word doc from Windows Explorer into the X-Change window and drop it there (or do **File** → *Open* directly from X-Change). It may take a few moments to process the entire file.

3. In X-Change, go to the **Organize Ribbon** and find the *Page Marks* section on the right. Click *Background* and choose *Add*.

Figure 202: Adding a background in PDF X-Change

4. Either choose your color or navigate to your background file. I recommend adjusting your background image opacity separately in Photoshop, then choosing 100% opacity in X-Change.

Figure 203: Background settings in PDF X-Change

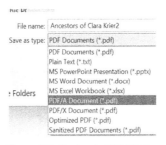

Figure 204: Saving in PDF X-Change

5. Save your file, making sure to select PDF/A as your "Save as type" rather than the "PDF Documents."

6. Admire your beautiful, properly formatted PDF.

LULU.COM SETTINGS

Here are the steps to having your book printed by Lulu.com. Most of these can be adjusted if you change your mind later, up until you actually order the book.

START

From the main Lulu.com page, go to the **Create** menu and choose *Print Books*. Then click the *Start My Print Book* button.

Figure 205: Starting a project on Lulu

SELECT A GOAL

You can leave your goal as "Print Your Book" for now and go back and change the answer later if you decide to make it available to other people.

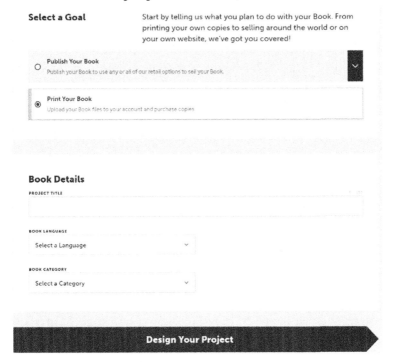

Figure 206: Goals and Details on Lulu

BOOK DETAILS

Fill in the title, language, and primary category (I like "Biographies & Memoirs") then click *Design Your Project*.

DESIGN

INTERIOR FILE UPLOAD

The first thing Lulu will ask for is the PDF that you exported. Drag and drop your file into the field. This step can take a long time – Lulu has to process every page of your book and make sure it complies with the requirements. Below is a screenshot of the page for uploading the interior file.

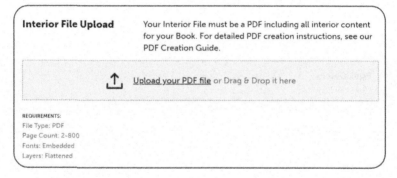

Figure 207: PDF Upload

You may get some error messages about transparent images, or images below 200 PPI. Personally, I ignore those messages and have not had any trouble yet.

When you get the green success message, you can move on.

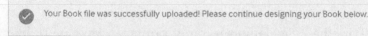

Figure 208: Successful upload message

BOOK SIZE & PAGE COUNT

You don't need to choose your book size or orientation, because Lulu will deduce this from the file you upload.

Figure 209: Book Size and Page Count

INTERIOR COLOR

Next you will choose whether you want color or black & white printing and whether you want standard or premium printing. I always recommend premium printing for books like this, when so many images are involved.

I prefer color printing for my own purposes, but I have begun making additional versions of my books in black & white for family members who prefer a lower price. Color is the most significant factor in the final price of the book.

PAPER TYPE

Again, I prefer premium paper, the 80# coated white, which is recommended if you choose premium printing. I don't have any issues with "see-through" pages when I choose 80#

paper, but I can't speak to that potential issue when using 60# paper. If possible, treat yourself to the premium options to celebrate all of your hard work on this project.

BOOK BINDING

This is the other major factor in determining book cost. I like hardcover for my own books. It looks very professional and makes an excellent impression. It also feels sturdier and like it can be handed down undamaged to future generations more easily than a soft cover.

One benefit of a coil-bound book is that the reader can open it and lay it flat. I find that very appealing as a reader when I need to take notes on someone else's book.

Paperback is a very economical choice when available. You may find some cover options are grayed out, because they are not available for your book size or page count.

COVER FINISH

This is an easy one – simply choose Glossy or Matte for your cover finish (I prefer Matte).

After you make all these decisions, you will see the price for printing your book. If it is not agreeable to you, you can go back and make different printing, paper, or cover choices to see a new print cost.

ADD A COVER (LULU)

A good cover helps your book appeal to possible readers and makes you smile every time you look at it.

Photographs are one of the most eye-catching elements you can include on your book cover. They help the people inside feel real and draw the reader into your story.

I like to include a fan chart on my back cover. There have been many times at research centers where I have been perusing other family history books and I saw one of my family surnames, so I picked that book up to see if it included my specific line. Answering that question often took a lot of page-flipping and skimming. I wanted my book to have a clearer and quicker answer.

The actual design of covers is beyond the scope of this project, but I will show some of the options Lulu offers.

LULU COVERS

Lulu provides several options for designing your book cover. Alternatively, you can choose a hardcover linen wrap with foil stamping.

UPLOAD COVER FILE

If you already have graphic design software that you like, you can design your own cover from the ground up.

Figure 210: Upload a cover file on Lulu

For a hardcover book, your cover file needs to include the back, the spine, and the front of the book. Most printers will offer a template you can download to make sure you are

Figure 211: Lulu cover template

creating a file with the exact specifications needed for a book of your size, number of pages, and selected paper thickness (the spine has to be the correct width). Pay attention to the different parts of the template, to make sure you don't put anything important in an area that could be trimmed away.

> Tip: Avoid the use of Artificial Intelligence image generators for your cover. Ethical and copyright issues are very complex when AI is involved, and your book may be rejected from sites such as Amazon.com.

PHOTOSHOP

I used Photoshop to create a general template for my book covers, one that I can adapt for each great-grandparent. I use layer masks to easily crop the photos. I took the parchment design that I used on the interior pages and made it the basis of the cover as well, with added color.

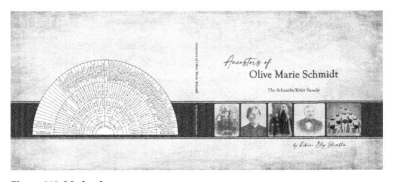

Figure 212: My book cover

Here is an example of my cover with the template overlaid (I imported it as a new layer and adjusted opacity). Notice how I made sure all of the text and images are inside the dark purple boundary. I also left enough space below my fan chart for a barcode should I need one.

Figure 213: Cover with template overlay

If you plan to sell your book via Amazon or similar distributors, you must leave room for a barcode on the back.

QUICK TEMPLATE COVER

Lulu offers ready-made cover templates. Simply fill in the book details, choose a template, upload an image, and pick a color.

This is the simplest solution if you are not comfortable with graphic design. It creates a clean, professional look with very little effort.

Figure 214: Lulu Quick Template Cover Info

PHASE 4: PRINTING

Choose a template

○ Two-color with image

○ Front cover image

○ Centered title

○ Spine image

Upload an image

Uploaded File   1902c BK-Magdelena,Lucy,Mathilda-Sebastian,Joseph,Peter-George f ront,Emma Meyer,Michel Kolbach.jpg

 Replace your image file or Drag & Drop it here

REQUIREMENTS File Type: jpeg or png

Review your Cover

Select a Color Theme

Figure 216:
Lulu
Upload
Cover
Image &
Pick Color

223

CANVA

Canva.com is a website that allows users to easily create graphic design elements. Lulu provides automatically-sized Canva templates for book covers, accessible when you click on the Canva link in the Cover Creator section.

Your project will automatically open in Canva with the correct dimensions needed for your book. This is very helpful, but it does mean that most of the free book cover templates on Canva will not work for you. You will be creating your cover "from scratch" in this case (but of course you can always look at the templates for inspiration).

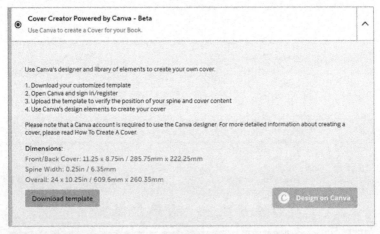

Figure 217: Canva Cover Creator from Lulu

Canva also offers premium templates for a small fee. Leave plenty of time to explore all of your options.

CREATE YOUR COVER

Finally, Lulu has a graphic design interface right on its website if you want more flexibility than the template offers.

Figure 218: Create Your Cover on Lulu

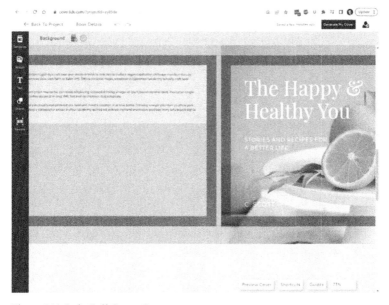

Figure 219: Lulu Full Cover Creator

PREVIEW YOUR BOOK

When you have successfully uploaded your PDF and uploaded or created your cover, you can preview the final product. Lulu will show you trim/bleed zones and margins, so you can make sure one final time that everything is laid out properly.

Do take the time to click through every page in your book. I cannot tell you how many times I thought everything was perfect, only to stumble on some strange formatting quirk that I had not seen before. This is your last chance to catch these issues.

When you are satisfied with your work, go ahead and order the book. Remember, you want to order only a single copy that will be your "Proof Copy."

PROOFS & REVISIONS

At this point, every part of you will want to declare this project *complete* and celebrate your victory. Please, resist the urge. Your masterpiece is not quite finished. You need to wait for the proof copy and look it over before it is really done. Yes, it seems perfect or you would not have clicked *Order*, but some things only pop out when you see them "in real life" on the page.

Tip: If you are creating this book for a family reunion or birthday party, *make sure* to leave time for this proofing phase.

When you finally hold the proof book in your hands, take a moment to savor all of your hard work. You are so close! Then get to work on your proofreading.

PROOFREADING

Look for issues with the following aspects of your book:

1. **Cover** – If your image is supposed to be centered on the cover, is it? Or does it need to be nudged over? Was anything covered up by a barcode?

2. **Spine** – Is your text centered properly on the spine? Horizontally and vertically?

3. **Page Trim** – If you have colored page backgrounds, do they go all the way to the edge of the page, or are there white strips? If there are problems, double-check your page settings (especially bleed) and talk to customer service.

4. **Color** – Do the colors on the cover look as you expected? How about the photographs inside? Translating from screen to print is a challenge in many cases.

5. **Font** – Is your font readable and properly sized?

6. **Formatting** – Did you remember to update all your indexes? Are the page numbers in your Table of Contents correct? Do all your images have captions?

7. **Content** – Does the book "flow"? Do your timelines make sense? If you have time, sit down and read the entire thing, cover to cover.

> Tip: Take notes on tiny things you would change if you had to do it again. Maybe each individual issue does not seem worth a reprint, but they can add up.

If you have read it too many times to see it objectively, try reading the book backwards, last page first. When your brain stops automatically filling in what it expects to see, some problems can come to light for the first time.

In fact, time can be your friend. If you are able, put the book down and don't look at it for an entire week. Then sit down with fresh eyes and scan your work again.

A SECOND PAIR OF EYES

Truly fresh eyes are only possible if you ask someone else for help. If there is an interested family member, recruit them to look over your proof and give feedback.

Be specific about the kind of criticism you are looking for, and what you can and cannot change at this point (e.g., "I can fix typos, but it is too late to add people to the book").

Don't throw away a "bad" proof. Even if you find many problems in your proof copy, do not get rid of it. Someone in your family might love to have it, problems and all. Perhaps your proofreader would appreciate this free copy.

CONSIDER A SECOND EDITION

As authors, we never stop wanting to improve. Even after you complete this process and have a final version, you may want to keep a list of possible revisions for a second edition.

You might store ideas in a physical notebook or a file on your computer. Personally, I have an email thread going with myself. Every time I think of something to add or change to my published works, I reply to my own email. This way when I sit down for a second edition someday, I will have everything at my fingertips.

What kind of changes do I have planned?

- Fix a typo in a caption that somehow slipped by my extensive editing process
- Replace a photo with a higher-resolution version
- Add names for people in an unlabeled photo
- Add indexing to the biographies in my first book
- Add a new family portrait I have unearthed

PHASE 5:
DISTRIBUTION

5

Once you have the final version ready, it is time to release your beautiful book into the world. That might mean ordering a final copy just for yourself, ordering multiple copies to hand out in person, or making arrangements for family members to order their own copies.

Remember, the goal of this project is to leave a strong legacy of your life's work. Don't let it languish on your own bookshelf. Share it with your family and the world.

GIVING AWAY COPIES

DISTRIBUTING PERSONALLY

If there are only a few family members who would be interested, handing out books personally is an incredibly satisfying thing to do. Seeing the look on someone's face when they first flip open the cover is an emotional thrill.

Considering video recording the moment someone opens your book. Every time I present a book to my grandmother, she immediately begins reminiscing and sharing stories about the people inside. Sometimes they are stories I have never heard! Certainly, there are tidbits that would be wonderful additions to any future editions of the book.

For family living too far away, you can still send emails and make phone calls, spreading the joyful news.

EMAILING A PDF

Not everyone wants or needs physical copies of content. As a photographer, I believe very strongly in leaving behind physical legacies for our grandchildren, but I acknowledge the role of digital content in this world.

So, you may have family members or fellow researchers who really just want a digital copy. You can send them the PDF in that case. Your favorite filesharing app (e.g., www.DropBox.com) can help with that. I love using www.WeTransfer.com to send large files for free, with no registration required. Or you might just save it to a USB drive and give them that.

DONATING TO ARCHIVES

Is your book focused on a certain geographical location, or cultural group? Perhaps there is a related historical society who would appreciate a copy of it. The only reason I even began writing my first book was that I had found someone else's in a research center (the Luxembourg American Cultural Center, to be exact). The thought that I could create something like this had never occurred to me. Maybe your book can be the catalyst for someone else.

This isn't even purely altruistic. Imagine being contacted by someone who found your book in an archive and wants to share their own research with you!

SELLING COPIES

Of course, printing is not free, and you may want to offer copies of your book for sale.

SELLING ON LULU

One big reason I chose Lulu as my printing company in the first place was the ease with which I could sell copies directly. Here is a step-by-step guide to getting set up.

START

Back when you first created the project on Lulu, you had the option to "Select a Goal." If you chose "Print Your Book," you saw only the tabs I have discussed already – Start, Design, and Review.

Figure 220: Basic tabs on Lulu.com

PHASE 5: DISTRIBUTION

You can revisit this Start tab and change your answer. When you change your answer to "Publish Your Book," new tab options will appear.

Figure 221: 'Publish Your Book' Goal on Lulu

If you are new to this process, stick with "Lulu Bookstore" for now. Those experienced in web design may also choose "Lulu Direct" to sell directly from their website.

If your book is of interest to the general public, you may add Global Distribution (e.g., Amazon.com), but that option is more complex and beyond the scope of this book.

COPYRIGHT

Since you are now selling your book, you will need to fill out some information concerning copyright. You will start with the Title, Subtitle, and Contributors. If you are working alone, you can just enter your own name here.

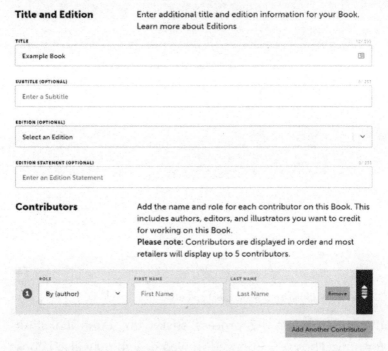

Figure 222: Title and Edition on Lulu

I always choose All Rights Reserved for my books, but you can choose to make your work available under a Creative Commons License or make it public domain.

PHASE 5: DISTRIBUTION

Copyright Select the copyright license that best suits your work. For more information about copyright, please see our Copyright Office FAQ

All Rights Reserved - Standard Copyright License
All Rights Reserved licensing. Your work cannot be distributed, remixed, or otherwise used without your express consent.

COPYRIGHT HOLDER NAME (OPTIONAL)

COPYRIGHT YEAR (OPTIONAL)

Some Rights Reserved - Creative Commons (CC BY)
Some rights are reserved, based on the specific Creative Commons Licensing you select.
What is Creative Commons?

No Rights Reserved - Public Domain
No rights are reserved and the work is freely available for anyone to use, distribute, and alter in any way.

Figure 223: Copyright on Lulu

Finally, Lulu will ask for an ISBN (International Standard Book Number). This is only required if you are planning to sell your book through Amazon or other global sellers. You can choose "Proceed without ISBN."

ISBN The International Standard Book Number (ISBN) is a unique identifier for your book. If you select Global Distribution, an ISBN is required.

ISBN Not Required
If you are only selling your book on the Lulu Bookstore, an ISBN is not required. You can add an ISBN at any time if you decide later to sell your book through retailers.

Use a free ISBN
Use a free Lulu ISBN with Lulu assigned as the publishing imprint. Once your Book is published and the proof is approved, the ISBN will never expire and remain attached to your published Book indefinitely.

I have my own ISBN
Add a previously unused ISBN to your Book

Proceed without ISBN

Figure 224: ISBN on Lulu

DETAILS

The next new tab concerns details about your book that are used for categorizing and selling it. Fill in a description of your book (what might be printed on the back cover in a store) and information about yourself. If you plan to sell your book on your website via Lulu Direct, this is the description that will automatically feed the book listing.

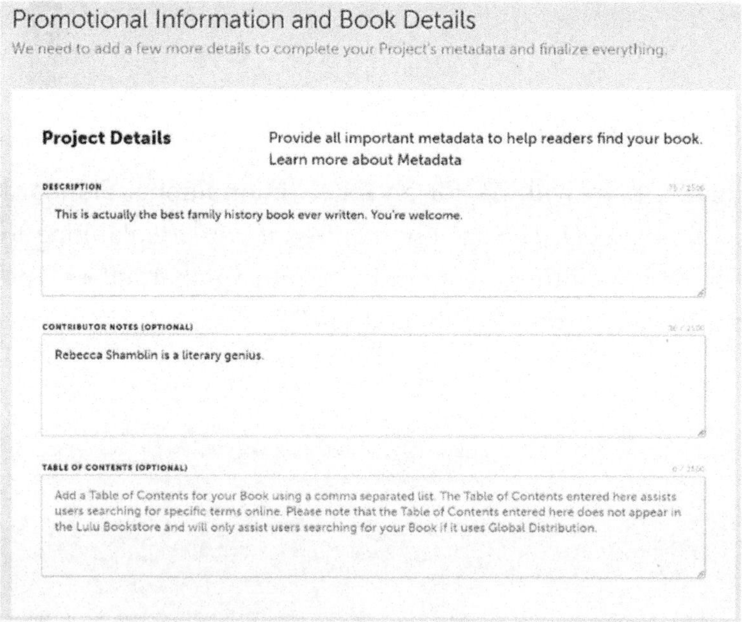

Promotional Information and Book Details
We need to add a few more details to complete your Project's metadata and finalize everything.

Project Details — Provide all important metadata to help readers find your book. Learn more about Metadata

DESCRIPTION

This is actually the best family history book ever written. You're welcome.

CONTRIBUTOR NOTES (OPTIONAL)

Rebecca Shamblin is a literary genius.

TABLE OF CONTENTS (OPTIONAL)

Add a Table of Contents for your Book using a comma separated list. The Table of Contents entered here assists users searching for specific terms online. Please note that the Table of Contents entered here does not appear in the Lulu Bookstore and will only assist users searching for your Book if it uses Global Distribution.

Figure 225: Promotional Information and Details on Lulu

You only need to fill in the Table of Contents if you are selling your book globally.

Categories and Keywords will help Lulu group your book with similar content.

PHASE 5: DISTRIBUTION

I usually use the category of "BIOGRAPHY & AUTOBIOGRAPHY / General" and then choose "History" for two geographical locations (where my ancestors immigrated from and where they settled).

I use Keywords to indicate more specifically what is mentioned in my book. I include surnames, county names, town names, and immigration-related words and phrases.

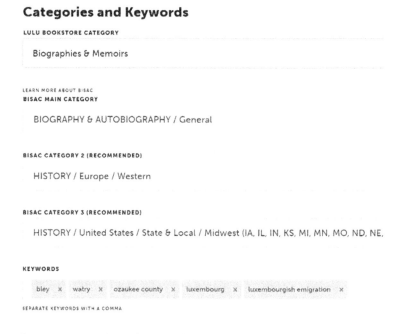

Figure 226: Categories and Keywords on Lulu

Finally, choose your audience and make sure to warn Lulu if your book contains explicit content. This seems unlikely in a family history book (depending on your family's occupations) but perhaps there are explicit descriptions of war and death in your stories.

Figure 227: Audience on Lulu

PRICING & PAYEES

The last new tab in Lulu concerns pricing and payees. How much will your book cost? And who will receive the profits?

You can determine your pricing in two ways. With a Fixed List Price, you simply tell Lulu how you want to price your book in each currency, and Lulu will let you know what the profits would be in that case.

Or if you set the pricing to be Revenue Goal, you just tell Lulu how much you would like to profit per book, and Lulu automatically calculates prices in various currencies.

PHASE 5: DISTRIBUTION

Set a Retail Price   Set the price for each currency manually or select a re'
goal for each Book sale.

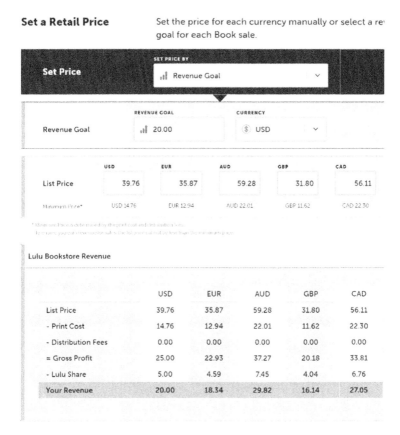

	USD	EUR	AUD	GBP	CAD
List Price	39.76	35.87	59.28	31.80	56.11
Minimum Price*	USD 14.76	EUR 12.94	AUD 22.01	GBP 11.62	CAD 22.30

Lulu Bookstore Revenue

	USD	EUR	AUD	GBP	CAD
List Price	39.76	35.87	59.28	31.80	56.11
- Print Cost	14.76	12.94	22.01	11.62	22.30
- Distribution Fees	0.00	0.00	0.00	0.00	0.00
= Gross Profit	25.00	22.93	37.27	20.18	33.81
- Lulu Share	5.00	4.59	7.45	4.04	6.76
Your Revenue	20.00	18.34	29.82	16.14	27.05

Figure 228: Setting Prices on Lulu

Once Lulu has made these calculations, you can edit the suggested prices to be whatever you want. I recommend either rounding to the nearest 5 or 10 dollars, or ending your prices with a "9," as in "$39" instead of "$40."

Finally, let Lulu know who to pay when people order your book. If you are the sole author, this is an easy answer. If you have been working with a family member, here is where you can allocate them their share of the profits.

241

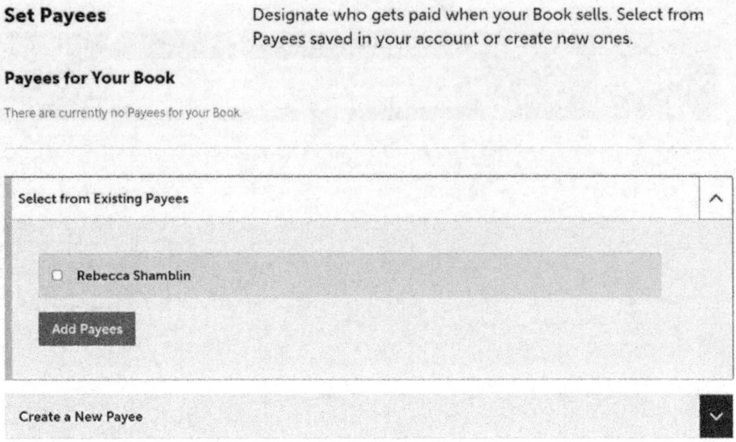

Set Payees

Designate who gets paid when your Book sells. Select from Payees saved in your account or create new ones.

Payees for Your Book

There are currently no Payees for your Book.

Select from Existing Payees   ∧

   ○ Rebecca Shamblin

Add Payees

Create a New Payee   ∨

Figure 229: Set Payees in Lulu

PRICING CONSIDERATIONS

When determining a price for your book, remember that your own expenses go far beyond the simple printing cost. Here are some expenses you may have incurred in the creation of your book:

1. Software purchases (such as Family Tree Maker)
2. Genealogy subscriptions (such as Ancestry.com or MyHeritage.com)
3. Database subscriptions (such as Newspapers.com or Archion.de)
4. Travel costs for in-person research and admission to record centers
5. Membership in various historical societies

6. DNA testing
7. Hiring a local researcher to track down undigitized foreign records
8. Educational costs (such as webinars or this book)
9. Scanning/printing costs for photos and documents
10. Equipment costs (such as laptop, camera, or printer)

And none of this accounts for your hundreds or thousands of hours of labor. Yes, we do this because we have a passion for it, and we love the work. But it is not a free hobby.

I don't know of anyone who has actually made a profit by writing a family history book. But it is fair to ask for a little help in recouping the costs of its creation.

SELLING ON YOUR WEBSITE

With my first book, I simply directed family members to the link on Lulu.com. Although certainly the simplest and easiest approach, the drawback to this method is that I had absolutely no visibility into who was buying my books. I could not see names or locations, and I certainly could not collect email addresses to notify people of future projects or help them if they had problems with their orders.

With the release of my second book, I invested a few days in learning about Lulu Direct and adding the WooCommerce plug-in to my website. With this method, I am able to see everything about each customer, better preparing me to answer questions from them (like, "Has my book shipped yet?") and let them know when my next book is ready.

Figure 230: My bookshop using Lulu Direct

I also have access to much better reporting, including "How many copies of each book have I sold?" (a simple question that the main Lulu shop portal seems surprisingly unable to answer easily).

Using Lulu Direct and website plugins is a highly technical process. I encourage you to make use of their knowledge bases and customer service if you go down this path.

OUTREACH

Once you have your ordering link set up (whether it is for your Lulu Bookshop page or your own website), it is time to let the world know. Here are some ideas for inviting people to see and order your book:

1. **Email fellow researchers working on your family lines.** During the research phase of my projects, I collect small groups of people working in similar areas so we can ask each other questions and share finds. When my book was finished, I had a perfect email list of people directly interested in my research.

2. **Message DNA matches**. It was a tedious and repetitive task, but I sent private messages to every relevant DNA match I could find. I prepared a short paragraph about the book, shared the link, and assured the recipient that I would not bother them again. Then I copied and pasted that content … a lot.

3. **Post in relevant Facebook groups**. There were multiple Facebook groups related to my books. Some of them were location-based, and some of them were culturally-based, since 75% of my ancestry is Luxembourgish. And some of them were focused on the software I used, FTM and FBC.

    i. Certainly, the last groups were the most enthusiastic and appreciative of what I had done.

I did not share those links to sell anything, but only to share my excitement and perhaps inspire their own work. *Make sure to gain permission* before posting in groups and follow all of their stated guidelines for self-promotion.

Family Book Creator Users

Figure 231: Sharing my book in the FBC User Group

4. **Share links and information in your online tree**. You can attach chapters to the specific people mentioned in your book, or include "facts" with a link to your book. You can also upload a photo of your book cover with info about the book, tagging the relevant ancestors, and it may appear as a Photo Hint to other researchers on Ancestry.com.

Figure 232: Upload a photo of the book to your tree

PHASE 5: DISTRIBUTION

5. **Share links and information in cooperative trees**. Sites like FamilySearch, WikiTree, and FindAGrave are places for researchers working on the same person to gather. Add a note to the person's profile with information about your book. Imagine how exciting it would be if you stumbled on a listing like this for your ancestor and discovered someone had already written a book!

Figure 233: Sharing my book on WikiTree

CONCLUSION

It is difficult to describe the feeling of holding your own book in your hands. It represents years of hard work and persistence, and you should be incredibly proud of your accomplishment.

Your book is a gift to yourself, your family, and future generations. Telling the stories of our ancestors is a time-honored tradition, and we are lucky to have the ability to record those stories and ensure that they remain long after we are gone.

You have my most heartfelt congratulations on achieving this milestone. Even if no one else in your family appreciates your efforts, know that the genealogical community is always ready to celebrate your work.

Hopefully, this is just Volume One in your amazing family history series. After all, we all know there is always more to find out there. Remember back in chapter one, when you had to pause researching? Good news …

SUPPLEMENTS

LETTER TO THE READER

Dear Reader,

I am so excited for you and your journey! Creating family history books has been one of the most rewarding accomplishments of my life. I can't wait for you to feel that same satisfaction and pride.

The book you are reading right now is a result of the incredible enthusiasm I received after sharing my first book in some of my genealogy communities. Person after person remarked that they had always wanted to do something like this, but didn't know how.

So I wrote a long blog post with tips, and presented several live workshops to share some of my strategies. But the questions kept coming! I realized that a book would be the best way to share everything I had learned and help others follow in my footsteps.

Teaching local and virtual classes about this content has also been incredibly rewarding and effective in helping people.

Did you find this book helpful? I *love* hearing from my readers, and I especially love seeing the beautiful books they produce. Please reach out and share your creations!

Love and luck to you,

Rebecca

ACKNOWLEDGEMENTS

I will always be grateful to the members of the Family Book Creator User Group on Facebook, especially moderator John Fassbender, who was the first person to invite me to teach my methods to others.

That group is also where I found my enthusiastic beta readers, including Digna, Taerie, Melinda, Diane, and Jane. Special thanks to my editors, Cathy Hanks and Sue Griffith, for their eagle eyes and attention to detail. Any remaining errors are definitely mine alone.

Stefan Harms, who created Family Book Creator, provided invaluable feedback for this project – no one knows his software like he does.

Finally, this project would not be what it is without the generous help and encouragement of other authors online, especially the Self Publishing Support Group.

AUTHOR INTERVIEW

How did you get started in genealogy?

Back in 2002, I was planning to attend a family reunion and meet many of my mom's cousins. I sat down to create a family tree so I could understand who the heck everyone was. Things got out of hand ...

How long does it take you to write a family history book?

Around 12-15 months. Keep in mind, I wrote the first two during a global pandemic, imprisoned in my house with two young children and nothing else to focus on. Your mileage may vary!

*Are you really going to write **eight** family history books?*

Nope, my goal is actually to write 12. I'd like to write ancestry books for each great-grandparent, then write descendant books for each set of great-grandparents. Dream big! Without stretch goals, we rarely stretch.

How do you spend your time when you manage to wrest yourself away from dusty genealogy records?

I am actually a portrait photographer with a studio near the Twin Cities in Minnesota. I specialize in babies and families, and my cheeks start to hurt every time I sit down to edit my photos because I can't help but smile at all those cuties on the screen.

252

SUPPLEMENTS

Do you sit in a chair all day?

I am a martial artist with a couple of black belts under my ... well, belt. I also try to start most mornings with a virtual reality workout called *Supernatural*. It's a blast!

What else do you do for fun?

I'm a big fan of *Outlander* (the books and the TV series), and I like to read romance novels (especially Nora Roberts).

Do your kids yawn when you babble about ancestors to them?

I have two daughters, ages 6 and 9, and they are extremely generous with me when I fall down genealogy rabbit holes. They smile and nod and hug me back when I jump up and down in excitement and exclaim over the 1785 baptism record I finally tracked down.

What are you writing next?

Thanks for asking, Imaginary Interviewer! The first project on my list is a companion workbook for this book, but then the world is wide open. What do you most want to read? Are there other genealogical questions you have? Feel free to write in with requests.

KEEP IN TOUCH

If you enjoyed this book, please subscribe to my mailing list and be the first to hear about any updates or new projects. You can sign up here: www.rebeccashamblin.com

You can also follow my page on Facebook: www.facebook.com/liferememberedgenealogy

Do you have questions about this material? Would you like to share your work with a community of people ready to cheer you on? Please join my Facebook group:

https://facebook.com/groups/rebeccashamblin

If you are wondering about something, chances are good that other people are wondering, too. Ask in the group so everyone can learn together. And who better to appreciate your hard work than other genealogists with the same dream? Come share your wins!

Did you find this book somewhere other than www.rebeccashamblin.com? Go check it out to download related products, including a Word template for narrative biographies and my FBC Settings file. You might even find some freebies there!

DISCUSSION PROMPTS

Is your local genealogy group or book club reading this book? Here are some questions to help guide your conversations:

1. What is the best family history book you have ever come across? What made it great?

2. What are the biggest obstacles you face in writing your own family book?

3. What do you think are the different challenges for writing an ancestry book *vs.* a descendant book?

4. How many generations feels like the right number to tackle in a single book?

5. What kinds of resources do you wish you had more access to in creating your book?

6. What are the pros and cons of creating printed books *vs.* eBooks? What do you prefer to read?

Please feel free to email me with questions, or even just a photo of your group meeting. I love to see readers interacting with my work.

I am also available for hire as a featured presenter at your next in-person or virtual meeting. Contact me at www.rebeccashamblin.com to learn more.

PRIOR PUBLICATIONS

90 Years of Sally (Kolbach) Feyereisen (2018)

Ancestors of Lawrence Casper Watry: The Watry/Weiland Family. (2021)

Ancestors of Olive Marie Schmidt: The Schmidt/Krier Family. (2022)

Printed in Great Britain
by Amazon